WEST DRAYTON & YIEWSLEY
through the centuries

A. H. Cox

West Drayton and District
Local History Society

HILLINGDON BOROUGH LIBRARIES
1983

Reprinted with Index 1995

© Hillingdon Borough Libraries 1983.
ISBN 0 907869 03 3
Designed by the London Borough of
Hillingdon Publicity Section.
Printed by Echo Press (1983) Ltd., Loughborough
for Hillingdon Borough Libraries,
High Street, Uxbridge, Middlesex.

FOREWORD

At the beginning of this century West Drayton must have been an idyllic place in which to live: on the rural Middlesex border with leafy Buckinghamshire, separated by a sweet flowing river, with fields and farms linked by quiet country lanes, the ancient church looking out upon the tranquil village scene. Around the village were fine houses for families who enjoyed country pursuits but were served by a fast and regular train service to London. The village cricket club boasted a titled member, Sir C. Aubrey Smith, a former captain of England, who subsequently went to Hollywood to become a character actor, specialising in playing roles as an English gentleman.

Although West Drayton, and neighbouring Yiewsley, have changed so dramatically in the second half of this century, there remains much of interest to local historians or readers curious about the area in bygone days. Fortunately there is no better or more knowledgeable guide than A. H. Cox, who has written this, the first history of West Drayton and Yiewsley from the earliest times to the present day. He has lived in West Drayton for over half-a-century and played an active part in community life. A founder member of the West Drayton and District Local History Society, he has been its Chairman since 1955.

When looking for an author to write this history there was no question of choice, it had to be A. H. Cox. I am delighted that he has responded to the invitation and that he has left for future generations the benefit of his knowledge and a record of his pride and affection for West Drayton.

Philip Colehan
Borough Librarian
London Borough of Hillingdon

CONTENTS

LIST OF ILLUSTRATIONS	6
INTRODUCTION	7
1. THE DISTANT PAST	9
2. THE DEAN'S MANOR c. 925–1546	10
3. THE PAGET ERA 1546–1786	12
4. THE DE BURGH ERA 1786–1918	18
5. ARMISTICE AND SECOND WAR 1918–1945	41
6. FROM VILLAGE TO SUBURBIA 1945–1982	57
EPILOGUE	69
SOURCES	70
FURTHER READING	72

ILLUSTRATIONS

Map of West Drayton area based on John Rocque's map of Middlesex, 1754	8
West Drayton Church	11
Gateway, West Drayton	13
West Drayton Post Office	16
'Irish Hovels', The Green	21
Padcroft College	23
West Drayton School Pierrots, 1905	26
New Church at Yiewsley, 1859	29
Map of West Drayton and district, early 19th century	32
Map of West Drayton and district, 1912	33
Empire Day, 1913	36
The Board Mill after the fire, 1913	37
The Swan Inn	40
The old blacksmith's shop, 1923	40
The old railway bridge, demolished in 1960	45
The Floating School, Yiewsley	47
The Central Hall, Yiewsley	49
The old Anchor Public House and blacksmith's shop which were demolished during the rebuilding of Colham Bridge in 1939	51
An outing from the Brickmakers' Arms in the early 1920's	53
Digging trenches at Yiewsley	55
Map of West Drayton and Yiewsley, 1982	61

INTRODUCTION

In 1941 the Vicar of West Drayton asked me to write a few short articles about St. Martin's Church for the parish magazine under the title "Peeps into the Past." This was something I had never attempted before and I found local historical research so intriguing that I have continued doing it ever since.

This small book does not claim to be a complete history of West Drayton, but within the space limits set me I have tried to give an outline of some of the events that have taken place in the past and to show how West Drayton and its neighbour, Yiewsley, have developed. In doing this I have used my own research notes of the past forty years and also the local history collection which the West Drayton & District Local History Society has accumulated since 1949.

My thanks are due to the Borough Librarian, Philip Colehan, his colleagues in the Libraries, Arts and Information Service, and also Tim Packwood of Brunel University for all the encouragement and advice they have given me in the preparation of this book.

A. H. Cox

Map

- Piel Heath
- 3 Houses
- Fill Potts Bridge
- Colham Green
- R. Colne
- Peeling Lane
- Royal Lane
- Colham Mill
- Goulds Green
- Paper Mill
- **WEST DRAYTON**
- Porter Lane
- Drayton Field
- Dawley
- Pinkwell
- The Lodge
- Harmondsworth
- Sipson Field
- Sipson
- Harmondsworth Field
- Harlington Field
- Harlington
- Heath Row Field
- Sipson Creek
- West End
- Kings Arbour
- Heath Row
- Shasbury Hill
- Cranford Field
- Cranford Bridge

Chapter One

The Distant Past

There are no written records of West Drayton until the tenth century, so we have to rely mainly on archaeological "digs" in and around the parish for its early history. Stone Age tools and Iron Age pottery have been discovered in local gravel pits. A large number of Palaeolithic stone tools have been found in gravel pits at Yiewsley, which is one of the richest of such sites in Britain. During the construction of Heathrow Airport fragments of Neolithic pottery dating to 2,000 B.C. and the remains of a temple (c. 500 B.C.) were uncovered. There is some evidence of the Roman occupation in the area. A Roman coin has been found at Harmondsworth and Roman pottery in archaeological "digs" at Larbourne Farm, Thorney in 1961 and at the rear of the Gate House in 1979-80. Research into a Roman trackway running from Verulamium (St. Albans) to Pontes (Staines) suggests that it passed through West Drayton at the Closes.

In prehistoric times much of southern England was covered by a forest belt in which small communities lived in clearings near a river. West Drayton is well supplied with streams, indeed its name (spelt Draegtun in its earliest form) means a place where a boat could be dragged over land — perhaps to avoid a bend in the river; but as The Green was a swamp in those days the houses would have been built on higher land, possibly on the hill that is now Church Road.

Yiewsley in early times was known as Wiuesleg (meaning wife's wood). It formed part of the Manor of Colham and lay within the Parish of Hillingdon. It was not until its rapid development during the 19th century that the history of Yiewsley and West Drayton drew closer together, resulting in the union of the two parishes into an urban district in 1929.

Until the nineteenth century West Drayton was isolated and its inhabitants would have had little contact with other villages. In all probability the earliest settlement was stockaded to protect it from the wild beasts living in the surrounding forest. The villagers had to be self-supporting; they farmed the land, hunted in the forest and fished in the rivers.

Following the Roman withdrawal in 410 A.D. the Saxon invasions seem to have made very little impact on West Drayton, probably on account of its isolated position. Towards the end of the ninth century, however, warfare did come very close to the village when a Danish raiding party was defeated at Farnham, Surrey. It fled northwards with its wounded leader and fortified itself on an island at Thorney. Here it was besieged by a Saxon force led by Alfred the Great's son, Edward. The siege ended in stalemate and eventually, after agreeing terms, the Danes withdrew. It must, however, have been a harrowing experience for the people of West Drayton to have had warfare on their doorstep; but after that the village was to enjoy over ten centuries of fairly peaceful existence until German bombs fell on it during the Second World War.

Facing:
Map of West Drayton area based on John Rocque's map of Middlesex, 1754

Chapter Two

The Dean's Manor c.925 – 1546

It is only from the tenth century that the history of West Drayton can be traced with any degree of certainty. King Athelstan (925 — 940) is reputed to have granted the manor to the Dean and Chapter of St. Paul's, and West Drayton thus became part of the church lands.

The Manor granted to St. Paul's comprised most of the parish of West Drayton with the exception of the part lying between Swan Road and Colham Mill Road, which formed a separate and smaller manor known as Drayton and Colham Garden. Little is known of this small manor, which was, in effect, little more than a large estate. Its manor house, known originally as Burroughs and later as Drayton House, was demolished in 1923. The fact that two manors, one large and the other small, lay within the parish of West Drayton had little effect on the development of the area, for their interests were similar and they both shared the same parish church.

The Domesday Survey of 1086 shows that the parish of West Drayton had 17 landholders, which suggests a population of under a hundred. There was a mill valued at 13s 5d (67p) and a weir at 32d (13p). The total value of the Manor was £6.

The Manor was managed on behalf of the Dean and Chapter of St. Paul's by an official known as a firmarius. He was responsible for the day to day running of the estate and had to see that produce in the form of corn, barley, oats, etc. was sent at regular intervals to the cathedral clergy and their staff. In addition West Drayton was obliged to pay twelve pence (5p in modern currency) as "Peter's Pence" — a tax payable to the Pope.

There is an early reference that William of Northall was the firmarius in 1181. In January of that year he was visited by the newly appointed Dean of St. Paul's, Ralph De Diceto, who was inspecting the manors that had just come into his possession. A report of this visit refers to the church, a priest and the priest's house.

The church would have been very small and perhaps of Saxon origin. It was replaced by a larger building in the 13th century, of which the base of the tower, the piscina and remains of lancet windows in the north chancel wall are incorporated in the present St. Martin's Church.

Roger of Worcester was firmarius of West Drayton at about the time of the building of the thirteenth century church, and a record of 1222 shows that the parish then had 630 acres of arable land, 16 acres of meadow and 8 acres of pasture.

Dean Ralph De Baldock visited West Drayton in 1297 and the inventory of the parish church then included two bells, four altars, six statues, a rood, a hanging enamelled pyx, a pewter chalice and a chest. The priest had two sets of vestments and his stipend was £2 per annum.

St. Martin's Church figures prominently in the history of West Drayton during the period when the manor was owned by St. Paul's. It was rebuilt again in the mid-15th century and one memorial from the earlier church has survived — part of a monumental brass to Richard Roos who died in 1406. He was a mercer and a citizen of London and owned the small Manor of Drayton and Colham Garden. Today St. Martin's Church stands as a reminder of the six centuries when West Drayton formed part of the estates of the Dean and Chapter of St. Paul's.

Towards the end of the era of the Dean's manor a new policy was adopted by St. Paul's. It no longer appointed a firmarius to look after its interests but instead leased the manor to a tenant. In 1525 a thirty year lease was granted by the Dean and Chapter to William Hyll. Twelve years later the lease was held by Robert Hyll who then assigned his interest in it to William Paget. The lease still had eighteen years to run, but possibly in order to secure continuity of tenure for his children Paget negotiated a new lease with St. Paul's and this was granted in 1540 for a term of sixty years.

It was by then the period of the Reformation and the confiscation of church lands. On April 1st, 1546 the Dean and Chapter surrendered their interest in the manor to the Crown. Fourteen days later Henry VIII granted the manor to William Paget.

West Drayton Church

Chapter Three

The Paget Era 1546 – 1786

William Paget was one of the most influential men of the Tudor period, holding high office under Henry VIII, Edward VI and Mary I. In 1544 he was knighted and five years later raised to the peerage as Baron Paget of Beaudesert, taking his title from an estate he owned in Staffordshire. He died in 1563 and is the first of many members of his family to be buried in the crypt of St. Martin's Church.

West Drayton was an ideal place in which to live for anyone connected with the royal household, for it was within comfortable distance of London, Windsor and Hampton Court. Indeed, there are memorials in St. Martin's Church to two royal servants — John Burnell (1551), who was Officer of the Cellar to Henry VIII, and James Eckersall who lived at Burroughs and was Clerk of the Kitchen to Queen Anne, George I and Chief Clerk of the Kitchen to George II. Paget appreciated his good fortune in living in West Drayton and referred to it in a letter to Sir William Cecil in 1551 in which he wrote "I wold not willingly be so long from seyng of my master his maieste beying so nere within v myles of my house."

While he was leasing the manor Paget was prepared to use the existing buildings, although he appears to have considered them inadequate for a man in his position. In 1538 he wrote to the Provost of King's College, Cambridge and in 1547 to the Earl of Warwick "from my *cotage* at Drayton." It is not surprising, therefore, that when he was granted the Lordship of the Manor he should have decided to build a manor house of a size that befitted a man of his status.

The old manorial buildings of St. Paul's (Paget's 'cotage') stood at the top of Church Road near St. Martin's Church and it was from this point that Paget developed his new home. His Manor House occupied much of the western end of the present churchyard, coming to within a few feet of the church tower and continuing southwards into what is now Beaudesert Mews. The grounds extended westward to the bottom of Church Road and were enclosed by a high Tudor brick wall, much of which still remains. The Gate House leading into the courtyard also survives, although altered considerably in appearance since Paget's day.

The building of the house and the laying out of its grounds must have made Paget extremely unpopular with the people of West Drayton. Many of them would have lived in small cottages in Church Road and these had to be demolished to make way for the manor mews and the pleasure gardens. In addition, the Manor House was built on the graves of generations of West Drayton people. Before the houses in Beaudesert Mews were erected, excavations carried out by archaeologists from the Museum of London revealed some of the foundations of Paget's mansion, a culvert, and over twenty skeletons of children, showing that at one time the churchyard had extended south of its present boundary.

The loss of the parish churchyard was offset by Paget's grant of an alternative burial site nearby. He accomplished this by the passing of a special Act of Parliament in 1550. This stated "the Vicar of the parishe church of West drayton in the Countie of Midd. and his successors and the inhabitants of this parishe of Westdraiton aforsaid for the tyme being shall and may have and enjoye forever one close of pasture in Westdraiton aforesaid called the Little grene Close at the townes ende contayning by estimation one acre." In return "the said William Lord Paget . . . . from the first daye of february shall have and enjoye forever to his and their own use and uses the churchyard of the parish church of Westdraiton aforesaid adioyning to the mansion house of the said Lord Pagett contayning by estimation three roods of ground." The Vicar, his successors and the inhabitants of West Drayton were given "forever free ingresse and egresse into and from the said parish church of West draiton." The alternative burial ground was in use until 1888 when it was closed by Order in Council. It lies within the grounds of Drayton Hall next to the Police Station, and some of the grave slabs still remain.

In addition to demolishing the houses in Church Road, Paget had also enclosed 150 acres of common land to form his demesne and had thus caused further discontent among his tenants. This he overcame in 1549 by signing an agreement with them under which they accepted his enclosure and he undertook not to enclose any more of the common land. The tenants were also granted the

Gateway, West Drayton

West Drayton & Yiewsley through the centuries

right of pasture on the waste lands of the manor. Finally, Paget legalised the position in the following year when he obtained a royal pardon for his actions in demolishing the houses and enclosing the land.

With the building of the Manor House it is possible to visualise the appearance of West Drayton as it was to exist with very little change for the next two and a half centuries. The other large mansion in the parish was Burroughs on the west side of Swan Road. South of this stood Rowtheys, the home of John Burnell, Henry VIII's Officer of the Cellar. It was destroyed by fire in 1778.

The slaughter house was in Myll Lane — that part of Money Lane running from St. Catherine's Rectory to Frays Close. The remainder of Money Lane did not come into existence until the West Drayton Enclosure of 1828. In Frays Close is the oldest house in West Drayton, Frays.

On the site of the maisonettes at the south west corner of The Green was Copts Corner, a Tudor farmhouse, later known as The Copse, which was demolished in 1966. Nearby, The Old Cottage still stands. A small farmhouse, Avenue Cottage, is now dwarfed by the adjoining Avenue House, which was built in the 18th century. South of it was another Tudor farmhouse on the site of the rear portion of Southlands. Palmers, now known as St. George's Meadows and a National Trust property, lies between Southlands and the river. It was the home of Thomas and Margaret Burnell. Margaret died on April 24th, 1529 and her monumental brass may be seen in St. Martin's Church. Other smaller cottages would have been on the higher ground around The Green, which was then the centre of the village and known as Town Street.

On Wednesday, Friday and Saturday copyholders had the right to fish in the rivers, on the banks of which were Oxeney and Hawthorne Moors. West Drayton Mill, on the site of an earlier mill mentioned in the Domesday survey, was enlarged by Lord Paget and in 1559 comprised two wheat mills and a barley mill.

South of The Green lay the common meadow land, Towney Mead, which has given its name to a local school. Drayton Field comprised about half the parish and extended from Porters Way to Cherry Lane. Here the copyholders cultivated their scattered plots. There was a rabbit warren at Coney Piece (now West Drayton Cemetery and the adjacent allotment land) and this provided food not only for the local poacher but also for the Paget household on whose menu rabbit was often an item. In 1568 Sir Henry Paget undertook to "supply sweet, reasonable and new taken coneys" to his mother, Lady Anne Paget.

The Reformation and its aftermath was a period of importance in the history of West Drayton. During the reign of Edward VI St. Martin's was the only church in Middlesex not to have had its pre-Reformation communion plate confiscated by the Crown. How it survived is not clear, but it could have been through the influence of Lord Paget that the church still owns this chalice and paten dated 1507-8, which was placed on permanent loan in the Diocesan Treasury in St. Paul's Cathedral in 1981.

Lord Paget and his successors were heavily involved in the political intrigues of their day. William Paget died on June 9th, 1563 and was succeeded by his son, Henry, who died only five years later without male issue. Henry's heir was his brother, Thomas, who thus became the third Lord Paget. Thomas Paget and his younger brother, Charles, were involved in the plot to assassinate Elizabeth I and place Mary, Queen of Scots on the throne. They were fortunate enough to have been abroad when the plot was discovered and there they remained in exile.

The Paget Era 1546-1786

In 1587 they were tried in their absence and deprived of their estates. West Drayton Manor thus reverted to the Crown.

Elizabeth I then granted the manor to her Lord Chancellor, Sir Christopher Hatton, and so West Drayton's connection with a royal courtier continued. On Hatton's death in 1591 the Queen gave the manor to her cousin, George Carey, Lord Hunsdon, and he it was who entertained her at the Manor House in October, 1602. This would have been a momentous occasion for the villagers, and one can imagine the scene as they waited outside the Gate House to see their queen pass through the gateway into the courtyard beyond.

Less than a year later, on September 8th, 1603, Lord Hunsdon died. In his will he left the sum of one hundred marks (about £66) for the benefit of the poor of West Drayton for ever. This is the oldest of the parish charities and the small income from it is still distributed annually on New Year's Day. Lord Hunsdon is buried in the family vault in Westminster Abbey, but in St. Martin's Church there is a small memorial which records "he was verie bountifuil unto the poore of this parish of West Drayton . . . . in thankful remembrance whereof the poore of this parish thought it meet to sett up this monument."

On the death of Lord Hunsdon, James I restored the manor to William, 4th Lord Paget, who had succeeded to the title when his father died in 1590. West Drayton then continued in the ownership of the Paget family for another century and a half.

There was much activity in the district during the Civil War. The 5th Lord Paget at first sided with the parliamentarians but later transferred his allegiance to the royalist cause, an act which resulted in a fine of £500 after the execution of the king. There seems to have been a fair amount of sympathy for the Roundheads in West Drayton, and John Biscoe, a Justice of the Peace who lived at Burroughs, was one of Cromwell's most ardent supporters.

During the Commonwealth marriage became a civil contract, and weddings took place before an official known as the Parish Register, and not in a religious ceremony conducted by a priest. From the marriage register of St. Martin's Church we learn that "John Daye was sworne and approved by me John Biscoe, Esq., J. P. to be Parish Register" on March 25th, 1654. John Baldwin was also a Parish Register in 1654 and he officiated when Richard Lees married Dorythe Skeirs of Iver on April 4th. Another Parish Register, John Washington, was "sworne and approved" on March 10th 1655. John Biscoe himself signed the register when William Child the Younger, gentleman of Chesham, married Mrs Katherin Smith on February 18th, 1657. The couple were evidently unhappy about the civil marriage, for the Vicar very courageously performed the illegal religious ceremony afterwards. This he recorded in the marriage register at the end of John Biscoe's entry — "and after by me, Emmanuel Hodges, Vicar."

After the exciting times of the Reformation and the Civil War, the remainder of the Paget period was one of comparative calm. In 1714 the 7th Lord Paget was created Earl of Uxbridge, a title now borne by the eldest son of the Marquess of Anglesey, the present head of the Paget family. Later the Pagets moved to Dawley and the Manor House apparently became derelict, for it was demolished c. 1750. In 1773 the site was acquired by Timothy Marshall and used for agricultural purposes.

Some of the houses built in the 17th and 18th centuries still survive around the Green. No. 15 was once the village stores and post office. In the mid-18th century it was owned by James Parratt and the churchwardens' accounts

West Drayton Post Office

The Paget Era 1546-1786

show that in November, 1754 they spent 2s 6d (12½p) on mops and brooms in his shop and 4s 1½d (21p) on nails in the following year. In 1766 the business was sold to John Haynes and it remained in the possession of his family for nearly two hundred years. John Haynes paid £26.0s. 10¼d (£26.04) for the stock and fittings. The original inventory survives and shows the variety of goods on sale in this small shop — "chese, rice, brushes, figdust, rossin, whomen's clogs, larde, treacle, oyle, sope, hocks of bacen" and much more. There was a brewhouse at the back and in the middle of the shop stood a brass 'furniss." As 6¼lbs of powder and 106 lbs of shot were stored close to this, it is perhaps surprising that the building survives today as a private residence.

Just beyond 15, The Green is the large wax factory of Messrs. Wilkins, Campbell, Ltd, formerly the Britannia Brewery, owned by the Thatcher family from 1805 until its closure c. 1911. Also in the complex were the Britannia Tap and the King's Head public house. The King's Head closed in the early 1930's.

Early in the 18th century George Cowdrey enlarged his Tudor farmhouse by building the Queen Anne frontage of Southlands. The Tudor building was replaced by the present rear portion of Southlands in the mid-nineteenth century. On the front of Southlands may be seen a Sun Insurance firemark bearing the policy number 95842. This policy was taken out in 1743 and it insured the house for £500 and the outbuildings for £300. The total annual premium was £1. 5s 0d (£1.25). Other houses in this area that have survived from the 18th century are Avenue House, Hope Cottage and No. 24, The Green.

On October 21st, 1786 the Earl of Uxbridge sold his interest in the Manor of West Drayton to Fysh Coppinger for £12,000. Thus ended West Drayton's connection with the Paget family, which had lasted, with one small break, for 240 years.

17

Chapter Four

The De Burgh Era 1786 – 1918

Fysh Coppinger was a lineal descendent of Hubert De Burgh, Earl of Kent and Grand Justiciar of England in the reign of Henry III. In 1790 he changed his surname to De Burgh. As the Manor House had been demolished, the De Burgh family made Drayton Hall their home, although on various occasions later they were obliged to let it furnished owing to their financial problems. Fysh De Burgh died on January 14th, 1800 and the Lordship of the Manor was then vested in his widow, Easter. On her death in 1823 it passed to her grandson, Hubert De Burgh.

Hubert's Lordship, which lasted nearly fifty years, saw the start of vast changes in West Drayton and Yiewsley after many centuries of mainly uneventful existence. De Burgh was a typical country squire, interested in hunting and pedigree horses and often in debt. He was an immensely unpopular Captain of the Uxbridge Yeomanry on account of his swearing. In 1863 the yeomanry refused to muster under his command at the celebrations in Uxbridge to mark the wedding of the Prince of Wales and Princess Alexandra of Denmark.

A few years later he entertained his friend, Napoleon III, the ex-Emperor of the French, at Drayton Hall, an event which is still recalled in the name Napoleon Cottages in Money Lane. A plaque, "Napoleon's Room," which was placed under a bell in the servants' quarters at Drayton Hall, still survives. There was a double door to Napoleon's room and tradition has it that this was fitted as a servant had been discovered listening at the key hole! Hubert De Burgh died on September 26th, 1872, aged 74, and the Uxbridge Yeomanry, of which he was by then the Hon. Colonel, escorted his coffin to St. Martin's Church where the 24th Uxbridge Rifles fired a salute.

The De Burghs also held the Manor of Colham, of which Yiewsley formed a part, and so, through their Lord of the Manor, West Drayton and Yiewsley shared a common interest which drew them closer together until they were united into an urban district in 1929.

POPULATION

At the beginning of the De Burgh period West Drayton and Yiewsley were still very isolated, lying midway between the two main outlets from London to the west — the Oxford Road through Uxbridge and the Bath Road through Harmondsworth. In 1811 West Drayton had a population of 555 and there were 109 houses in the parish. No separate figures are available for Yiewsley, which then lay within Hillingdon Parish. Fifty years later West Drayton's population had increased to 948 and the number of houses had risen to 185. The expectation of life was much lower than it is today; indeed, in 1866 the average life span was stated to be only 33 years. At West Drayton's celebration of Queen Victoria's

The De Burgh Era 1786-1918

Diamond Jubilee in 1897 there was a dinner for all the old folk in the village and everybody over forty was invited. Fourteen years later, at George V's Coronation celebrations, people were evidently living longer, for invitations were sent to everyone over fifty.

THE WEST DRAYTON ENCLOSURE

The appearance of West Drayton altered completely with the enclosure of common land in 1828. Until then the district had remained very much as it had been since the time of the first Lord Paget, nearly three hundred years before. It was not, however, an economical way of using agricultural land. Individual holdings were scattered over a wide area and so time was wasted travelling from plot to plot. In addition, there was a considerable wastage of land as paths wide enough to allow for the passage of a plough had to be left between the plots. Consequently the need arose for copyholders to have their land in one piece instead of several scattered plots. This was accomplished by Parliament passing the West Drayton Inclosure Act in 1824, and Thomas Denton of Ashford was appointed Commissioner to carry out its provisions. His task was to measure the plots and allot the same area to each copyholder, to see that the new allotments were fenced or hedged and to set out new roads and drains. All this he accomplished by 1828. The Green was to remain unenclosed and the right of grazing beasts on it was forbidden.

TRANSPORT

At the end of the 18th century the canal was cut through the district forming a visible boundary between the two villages. Today members of a few old Yiewsley families still refer to the canal as "the cut." The canal opened up the district for trade as it provided a cheap, if slow, means of transport. On its banks were erected various wharves and industrial premises of which Colham Wharf, erected in 1796, survived until 1982. Work started on constructing the Slough arm of the canal in 1879 and West Drayton men refused to carry out the work at the wage offered to them of 18s 0d (90p) per week. The canal company responded by bringing in unemployed men from Suffolk who were glad to accept this amount.

Then in 1838 came the opening of the Great Western Railway with West Drayton as the first station out of Paddington. The original station was in Tavistock Road near the entrance to the coal depot and it was moved to its present site in 1879. A magazine article in 1838 describes the journey from Paddington to West Drayton and a stroll round the village. As the train arrived, West Drayton children from the British School were just leaving "from the path which led to knowledge, showing by their joyous activity and vociferation their delight at being freed from restraint". Opposite the school was a beer house (The Engine) "whence, even at this time of day, the stupid exclamation of rustic inebriety polluted the ear." On The Green, geese, pigs and donkeys grazed (thus breaking the conditions of the West Drayton Inclosure Act) and "many a pretty face was protruded from an upper casement to gaze upon us as we passed" for strangers were then a rarity in West Drayton. At the Swan Inn an excellent meal could be obtained in the upper room and "the interior exhilarated with a glass or two of sherry."

A branch line to Uxbridge opened in 1856 but was closed under the Beeching Plan in 1962. Another branch was opened to Colnbrook in 1884 and then extended to Staines. This line closed to passenger traffic in 1965. Until the opening of the railway the only means of transport was on horseback or by horse-drawn vehicles. The stage coach could be boarded at Uxbridge or on the Bath Road and carrier services to London were run by Thomas Pewsey, John Cock and Thomas Stevens.

THE BRICKFIELDS AND OTHER EMPLOYMENT

The two main industries in the district during the 19th century were agriculture and brickmaking. In 1861 there were 121 agricultural workers in West Drayton, of whom twenty-two men and a boy worked for William Batt, who farmed four hundred acres. In Yiewsley there were 117 agricultural labourers, most of whom would have been employed by William Studds at Philpotts Farm (120 acres) or by William Roadnight at Rabbs Farm (228 acres). The brickfields provided jobs for 163 Yiewsley men but only twelve from West Drayton. Edward Fountain, a mealman of Yiewsley, employed thirteen men and a boy. Other sources of employment in 1861 were in oil cake manufacturing and at the varnish works in Yiewsley, and at Thatchers' Brewery and the Mercer family's mill at West Drayton. The main source of employment for women was in domestic service. In 1868 a general servant would be paid £8 per annum and a cook £10. Some women, however, worked at home as dressmakers, milliners or laundresses. In addition there were numerous shopkeepers and publicans.

     The district, especially Yiewsley, was rich in brick earth and much of 19th century London was built of bricks made in Yiewsley, Starveall (renamed Stockley in 1912) and West Drayton, the bricks being carried to the capital by barges on the canal. The growth of the brickfields resulted in an increase of the population of Yiewsley, which is thus very much a development of the 19th century.

     But although the brickfields provided such a large amount of employment the conditions and pay were exceedingly bad. It was a seasonal occupation and work lasted for only about four months in the summer. Unless he could find other employment the "brickie" was in very straitened circumstances for the rest of the year. Those who could afford it reared a pig in their back garden in order to provide meat and bacon in times of hardship and this was known as the "brickmakers' bank".

     The "brickies" worked in gangs known as stools consisting of a moulder, an off bearer, temperer and four boys. In 1891 the total weekly wage of a stool of seven amounted to £5.16s 8d (£5.83). They were staunch supporters of the National Union of Brickmakers and Gas Stokers, and after a meeting on West Drayton Green in 1890 seventy eight new members were enrolled.

     There were frequent and damaging strikes. In 1890 they struck over the employment of non-union labour. At Eastwood's brickfield an employee whose union membership had lapsed had to be dismissed before the men would go back to work, while at Rutter's three men were forced to join the union in order to stop the strike. In the following year the brickfields were on strike for seventeen weeks over a wage dispute. The employers offered 4s 4d (21½p) per thousand bricks "ground on table" or 4s 8d (23p) per thousand "in pug hole". The men demanded 4s 10d (24p) and 5s 2d (26p). The local M.P., Sir F. D. Dixon-Hartland, and the Vicar of Yiewsley, the Rev. H. Francis, tried hard to bring the two sides together. Eventually the strike collapsed. In July the men at Eastwoods' brickfield returned to work and in August the union decided to leave

The De Burgh Era 1786-1918

'Irish Hovels', The Green

it to the men to make their own decision. Some went back to work, but others stayed out as the season was by then nearly over.

The brickfields never really recovered from this strike and in 1906 Rutters were forced to reduce the wages of the men from £1. 6s 0d (£1.30) per week to £1. 4s 8d (£1.23) and of boys from 7s 0d (35p) to 6s 8d (33p) owing to the depression. The brickfields were gradually worked out and the final field closed in 1935. As the brickfields were declining, however, other industries were being established in the district, such as the Power Plant Co., the Rotary Photographic Co. and Wilkins Campbell, Ltd.

POVERTY

There was much poverty throughout the district during this period. Paupers were a charge on the parish, and if it could be proved that a destitute person came from another district he would be returned there in order to avoid paying relief money. Thus in 1766 the West Drayton churchwardens spent 10s 0d (50p) for "conveying the Allwright family to their parish" rather than pay considerably more in relief if they had been allowed to stay in West Drayton. In 1841 Catherine Pearce was sent to West Drayton by the Harmondsworth Overseers of the Poor as it was claimed she belonged to West Drayton parish. This was disputed by the West Drayton Overseers who gave notice of appeal against the order. There were other ways in which the poor could be helped besides giving them money, and in 1771 the West Drayton churchwardens had paid 5s 0d (25p) on "bead and beading for John Holmes." After the Napoleonic Wars the calls on the parish for poor relief increased and by 1819 West Drayton's poor rate had risen to 1s 6d (7½p) in the £. Later things improved and by 1840 the poor rate had fallen to 2d (1p).

In 1807 a workhouse was erected in West Drayton and much of it still remains as Nos. 1 — 7 (odd numbers) The Green (No. 9 was rebuilt in the 1950's). Details of the building costs show that a total sum of £289. 19s 5d (£289.92) was spent on erecting this building. Of this, Hill and Gunn, two labourers, received 12s 6d (62½p) between them for five days' work, but this low wage seems to have been more than compensated by the next item which reads "beer for the workmen £1. 1s. 10½d" (£1.09). This building remained the parish workhouse until 1838 when the inmates were transferred to the Uxbridge Union Workhouse, parts of which survive in Hillingdon Hospital.

Court cases sometimes reflect the poverty of the 19th century. In 1862 thirteen-year-old James King was charged with stealing a piece of cheese from a sandwich belonging to a porter at West Drayton Station. His mother was a widow with three children and received 2s 0d (10p) a week and three loaves in parish relief. Despite an appeal from the boy's young sister he was sent to a reformatory for two years. At an inquest in 1906 the parents of a ten-year-old Yiewsley girl, who had died of bronchitis and exhaustion caused by lack of nourishment and attention, were censured. There were six children in the family and the father's weekly wage varied from 14s 0d (70p) to £1 a week. His wife paid 5s 3d (26½p) a week rent out of the housekeeping money and the man kept 2s 0d (10p) a week for himself which he spent on drink.

Various efforts were made throughout the district to alleviate the plight of the poor. There were coal and clothing clubs, often financed by the better off members of the community. Working men's clubs were established in both villages and the sick were cared for by the Yiewsley district nurse who made 1161 visits to Yiewsley and 560 in West Drayton during 1906. Unemployment increased in the winter months when the brickfields were closed and bad weather would prevent agricultural work being carried out. During periods of very bad weather, soup kitchens were opened by Mrs Cosmo Hamilton at "Southlands" and by Mr. & Mrs. Liddall in their coach house in St. Stephen's Road. Publicans, too, would assist in this work and in 1905 Mr. and Mrs. Cox of "The Crown," West Drayton provided a substantial dinner consisting of meat and three vegetables twice a week for fifty poor people at a cost of only 2d (1p) for adults and 1d (½p) for children.

SCHOOLS

Until the passing of the 1870 Education Act the state took no part in the provision of schools. Consequently the early schools in the district were either privately owned or run by the church.

The earliest reference to a private school occurs in Pigot's Commercial Directory for 1826 which lists James Webster's Gentlemen's Boarding Academy at West Drayton. Perhaps it was James Webster or a member of his staff who fell into the river in 1823 when the churchwardens "gave men assisting to get the schoolmaster out of the water 1s 6d" (7½p). Although this mishap occurred in the middle of the summer the schoolmaster seems to have developed a heavy cold, for the next item reads "Flannel for schoolmaster 1s 0d" (5p).

There were several small private schools held in houses or cottages. One such school is known to have existed on The Green in the 1870's and was run by Dame Whittington. At the same time the Misses Butler had their Establishment for Young Ladies at Harewood Villa, Yiewsley. Its curriculum included pianoforte, singing and the "usual branches of an English education." The fees

The De Burgh Era 1786-1918

were 15s 0d (75p) per quarter. By the 1890's Mrs J. W. Hardy, "assisted by professors and mistresses" had opened her Ladies' High Class School in De Burgh Crescent, West Drayton, where instruction was given in four languages, the playing of four instruments, art and dancing at moderate fees. Towards the end of the 19th century Miss Wakeford's Girls' School in Tavistock Road, Yiewsley received resident, weekly and day pupils.

In 1906 came the Berta School for Boys in Edith Villa, High Street, Yiewsley under Mr. Charles Richards, who had been mathematical tutor to the late Prince Imperial. Earlier Beaufort House School had been opened by Miss Brown in Vine House, The Green in 1888. It does not appear to have been very successful for it had closed within two years. The Women's Institute Hall was erected on its site in 1951.

Padcroft College

The most important of the private schools was *Padcroft College* which opened on October 4th, 1875 on the site of the present Heathcote Way flats. At one time the college had a hundred pupils, some of them boarders paying forty guineas a term, the fee for day boys being two guineas. The pupils were taught divinity, four languages, mathematics, natural science, drawing and "other branches of a liberal English education." There were four acres of playing fields, for sport played a prominent part in the college's life. Discipline was very strict. Padcroft College continued until the beginning of the present century when the building was sold to the Church of England Temperance Society for use as a home for "boys of the hooligan class." The home was later transferred to the London Police Court Mission and was closed in 1949.

Most of the children, however, attended one of the church schools in the district. The oldest of these was the *British School* near the railway bridge in Station Road. This was built by the British & Foreign Schools Society at a total cost of £482. 14s 11d (£482.75) and catered for the needs of the free church children. The school opened on January 7th, 1828 and at the end of its first year had a roll of one hundred and twenty pupils. The headmaster's salary was £25 per annum plus the pupils' fees. At first only boys were admitted, but in 1832 it was decided to make it a mixed school as it was considered that "the education of females was quite equal in importance to that of the male sex and perhaps more so, in as much as the training of children in the first stages of life follows principally the guidance of females." As a result of this decision the school was enlarged and a cottage was built for the master and mistress. In 1863 there were over two hundred pupils, but by 1891 this had declined to a hundred and twenty-one. The school closed c. 1903. Two beautifully written exercise books of 1857 and 1858, the work of William Brient, a pupil who was born in 1848, and also a sampler worked by Harriet Ransley in 1852, have survived. The school building was demolished in 1959.

West Drayton National School (Church of England) was opened by the National Society in 1859 on the site of the present West Drayton Library where its name plaque may be seen in the boundary wall. The first teachers, Mr. & Mrs. Styles, received a joint salary of £60 per annum plus the school house and fuel. By 1886 the joint salary had been increased to £140 per annum. *St. Catherine's School* for the Roman Catholic children started in a cottage in Money Lane but by 1868 had transferred to buildings at the back of St. Catherine's Church. The old school buildings are now used as part of the church club. At first the average attendance at the school was eighty but by 1877 this had fallen to forty-eight.

The foundation stone of *St. Matthew's School* was laid by Bishop Claughton in August, 1871 and the school opened on April 8th, 1872. The mistress of the infants' and girls' department, Harriet Veal, commented in her log book "Opened this school this morning with 38 children. Found them exceedingly backward, many of them never having been to school before . . . The whole of the children are very troublesome." Many of the children attending this school came from the Starveall (Stockley) brickfields area and eventually, in 1889, a small school was opened there for the children living in that part of the parish. Messrs. Broad, Harris & Co., one of the brickmaking firms, contributed £50 towards the cost of the building. Miss Dixon was appointed mistress and remained at the school until it closed in 1922.

The church schools provided most of the educational facilities for the district during the 19th century and two of them still remain. Some of the children were very young indeed and the 1861 census records many "scholars" aged two years. All the schools shared similar problems — finance, absenteeism, staff difficulties, pupil (and sometimes parental) misbehaviour, and these difficulties were recorded in the school log books.

The schools were usually staffed by a master and a mistress assisted by two or three student teachers who were aged between fourteen and sixteen. The student teachers received instruction from the master each morning between 7 and 8 a.m. before undertaking their duties. Sometimes an older pupil would be appointed monitor and would teach in the infants' class. In 1884 Kate Catermole, who was only ten, was put in charge of a class of very young children at St. Matthew's School.

The De Burgh Era 1786-1918

Until the introduction of compulsory free education in 1891 each pupil paid a fee of 2d (1p) per week but often these payments were in arrears. In November, 1873 William Goodman of St. Matthew's School was sent home for his school pence and it was then discovered that he had spent it on his way to school. In June, 1874 arrears at St. Matthew's School totalled 6s 8d (33p). Sometimes payments were in arrears from the Uxbridge Board of Guardians, who were responsible for the fees of the workhouse children attending the school. In 1875 the Guardians were two quarters overdue in their payments.

Absenteeism was often caused by children staying away to work in the brickfields, in gathering snails from growing crops or on farms during haymaking and harvest time. When the brickfields re-opened in March, 1874 three boys left West Drayton National School in order to work there. In May, 1894 fourteen boys from St. Matthew's were working in the brickfields although they had not obtained the necessary labour certificate, a fact which the headmaster reported to the brickfield managers. The school attendance officer, however, declined to prosecute the parents in this case. When the brickmaking season ended the absentees would return to school for the winter. But other children would stay away during very bad weather as they had no boots to wear and could not come barefoot through the snow.

There were, however, less valid reasons for absenteeism, such as the meetings at the West Drayton Race Course. In June, 1876 St. Matthew's School was obliged to close for a week "on account of the races which take place on Monday and Tuesday and to which the greater part of the school go." Later, West Drayton Golf Club attracted pupils for they could earn 6d (2½p) a day acting as caddies. Thirty five pupils were absent from St. Matthew's School on November 1st, 1898 and nine of them were seen on the golf course by a boy who was sent by the headmaster to find them. Annual fairs at West Drayton and Uxbridge affected the attendance and on October 13th, 1881 forty-six boys failed to return to St. Matthew's School in the afternoon when Sanger's Circus was at Uxbridge.

The children were taught arithmetic, spelling, handwriting, grammar, geography and singing. In addition the girls had needlework and knitting lessons. The Inspector's annual reports show not only the standard of education reached but also some of the difficulties the teachers faced. In 1882 West Drayton National School was "conscientiously worked" but half the school failed in arithmetic and dictation. The infants were "too listless and fidgety and can only with difficulty be induced to work." Two years later the infants were "rather talkative and somewhat inclined to copy" while in 1886 "the upper classes, especially the girls, shew remarkable density of intelligence." In 1888 the Inspector found "the needlework of the girls may pass as good, but darning must improve. The children seem to me to be teachable, though dull, especially the girls." The following year there was an improvement, while in 1890 "the school is pleasantly worked with fairly successful results." But in 1891 the Inspector found that reading was monotonous, the letter H was neglected and recitation was gabbled. There was much dullness and "I am sorry to have to take notice of copying." By 1893 "the first class copy from one another when not physically prevented." However, in 1896 a great improvement was noted, but "spitting on the slates must be strictly forbidden." A report on Starveall School in 1916 commented "the children are bright, happy and keen over their work. The teaching is faithful, spiritual and thorough with excellent results."

As the population expanded the church schools found it difficult to

West Drayton & Yiewsley through the centuries

West Drayton School Pierrots, 1905

meet the increased demand for places. In 1905 the Middlesex Education Committee opened two schools in Yiewsley and one in West Drayton and the district thus had its first "council schools." The Yiewsley Schools no longer exist, St. Stephen's now forming part of St. Matthew's School and Providence Road closing in 1981. The building of the West Drayton school was opposed by the Parish Council without success. It opened on August 28th, 1905 as the West Drayton Infants School with ninety-seven names on its roll and Mrs. M. M. Turner as headmistress. The site of one and a half acres next to the National School had been bought for £300 and the school was erected by Messrs. Henry Knight & Son of Tottenham at a cost of approximately £4,000. Later renamed West Drayton Primary School, it was transferred to the former St. Martin's School building in Kingston Lane in 1979 and the Station Road site was developed as a housing estate in 1982.

THE CHURCHES

Until 1827 *St. Martin's* was the only church in the district. Although Yiewsley people may have attended Sunday services there it was not their parish church, so for weddings, baptisms and funerals they had to go to St. John the Baptist, Hillingdon.

St. Martin's was surrounded by a high brick wall erected by Lord Paget c. 1550. In 1849 the Rev. J. H. Sperling visited the church and noticed its dilapidated condition. The tower was covered in ivy and its windows gutted. From the roof hung emblazoned banners, helmets, coronets, gauntlets and spurs but large quantities of other armour had been stolen over the years. Two large

The De Burgh Era 1786-1918

canopied pews were at the west end. There were remains of screens in the aisles suggesting that at one time there had been side altars. The font had a flat board cover fastened by staples. At about the same time that Sperling wrote his description of the church, an artist, O. Hudson, sketched some mediaeval stained glass windows in it and his drawings are now in the Victoria and Albert Museum.

It is indeed fortunate that we have these descriptions of St. Martin's in the mid-19th century, for shortly afterwards (1850-52) it underwent a drastic restoration and much that was of historic interest in it was either removed or ruthlessly destroyed. Anything connected with the Pagets disappeared, including the east window depicting their coat of arms and also some grave slabs which were smashed and used as rubble beneath the Victorian tiled floor laid by the "restorers." In 1849 Mr. Charles Grimes prepared a specification of the work required to be carried out and the estimate of Messrs. Fassnidge & Son of Uxbridge amounting to £512 was accepted. This sum did not include the cost of restoring the chancel which was the legal responsibility of the Lord of the Manor. £500 was borrowed from the Public Works Loan Office at 5% interest in 1850 and a further £190 two years later. In 1856 Hubert De Burgh restored to the parish part of the original churchyard west of the tower on which Lord Paget had built his Manor House three centuries before. The churchyard was extended further in 1905 when the Bishop of Kensington consecrated the northern section. By then the old burial ground at Drayton Hall was no longer in use.

On October 3rd, 1865 St. Martin's became one of the first buildings in West Drayton to be lit by gas and this was stated to give "the fine old edifice a very grand appearance." Evidently this was quite an innovation in the district, for the railway station was still poorly lit by oil lamps.

The Rev. Robert De Burgh, brother to the squire, was Vicar of West Drayton from 1844 until 1879 and up to 1866 he was also Vicar of Harmondsworth. The two benefices had been united in 1755 and most of the vicars lived in Harmondsworth, for there was no vicarage in West Drayton until 1888. Robert De Burgh lived at the Gate House, which was then known as The Lodge, and he was very much a sporting parson. After his retirement he joined the Roman Catholic church, of which his wife was a member, and this explains why he was buried in the churchyard and not in the family vault beneath the chancel when he died on December 27th, 1884 aged 83.

At that time the vicar's stipend was £300 per annum. In 1888 a house standing on the site of the present church hall was acquired as a vicarage at a cost of £720. It was demolished in 1962 after the present vicarage had been erected in its grounds.

The Rev. A. W. S. A. Row was the first vicar to live in the newly acquired vicarage, but later in his long incumbency (1889 — 1928) he let the house, which was then renamed "The Grange", and lived in The Gate House. His ministry of nearly thirty-nine years saw vast changes in the parish. In 1889 the population was small. There was very little street lighting and no main drainage or piped water supply. Traffic was horse drawn and there was one resident who still rode a penny-farthing bicycle. When he retired in 1928 Mr. Row could see that his parish was developing rapidly from a small agricultural village into a London suburb. Motor cars sped through its streets, several people had wireless sets and overhead could be seen the occasional aeroplane. Possibly he regretted these changes. In 1926, when he was presented with a cheque for a hundred guineas to mark his golden jubilee as a priest, he commented that in 1889 there were less than a thousand people living in West Drayton and so he was able to know them all, but alas, that was no longer the case. Yet in 1926 there were still only four hundred and fifty houses in the village.

St. Martin's prospered during Mr. Row's ministry. The Sunday School had a hundred and forty members in 1893 and it met both in the morning and the afternoon. Then in 1910 the morning service was so crowded that the vicar was obliged to introduce another service at 10 o'clock "as the pressure at the 11 o'clock service (strongly in evidence by the unseemly struggle for certain seats) needs relieving."

In 1817 some Uxbridge residents were concerned "at the destitute condition of the village of West Drayton and its neighbourhood as to the religious instruction which could make wise unto salvation" and as a result they started a Sunday School in the village. Later, Mr. Brown, a deacon of Uxbridge Independent Church, conducted Sunday evening services for adults and on his death in 1825 these services were continued by various Baptist ministers. By then the Sunday School attendance was a hundred and thirty five. In 1826 it was felt that a *Baptist* congregation could be formed in the village and that a chapel should be erected. The chapel opened in Money Lane in June, 1827 and here the Baptists worshipped until transferring to their present church in Swan Road in 1925. On September 25th, 1827 Mr. Andrew Gunton Fuller was elected first pastor. By 1839 the debt on the chapel had been cleared and it was then extended 18ft westward and a classroom was provided at a cost of £300. 0s 1d (£300.0½). This amount had been paid within four years.

Land was bought for a mission chapel in Trout Road for the people of Yiewsley. This little chapel cost £162. 10s. 10d (£162.59) to build. It opened in 1842 but was closed in 1867 as it was considered "now very nearly useless." Thirty years later, however, West Drayton Baptists re-opened their work in Yiewsley and this resulted in the formation of a separate Baptist congregation and the opening of *Yiewsley Baptist Tabernacle* in Ernest Road (now Colham Avenue) in 1900.

The Baptists fought hard to resolve the drink problem which beset West Drayton during the 19th and early 20th centuries. "The first painful case of discipline for intoxication" had occurred in 1829 and the offending brother whose "deportment during sermon time was observed to be peculiarly strange" confessed that "he had taken more than did him good" while in the King's Head. The male members of the church agreed "that it was the manifest tho' painful duty of the church to exclude him from communion." The drink problem still remained early in this century. The Salvation Army band would play outside the public houses in an attempt to lure the men away from the bars and then lead them to a midnight service in the chapel. This seems to have been very successful and sometimes as many as a hundred and fifty men and helpers would be present at a service.

By the middle of the 19th century the population of Yiewsley had increased so much that a chapel of ease, built to the design of Sir Gilbert Scott, was dedicated on July 6th, 1859. This little building is now the north aisle and chapel of *St. Matthew's Church*. It was staffed by curates of St. John the Baptist, Hillingdon which was still the parish church. In 1874 Yiewsley became a separate ecclesiastical parish and so the chapel of ease became a parish church with the Rev. A. E. Seymour as its first vicar. Yiewsley, however, still remained part of the civil parish of Hillingdon until 1896.

The De Burgh Era 1786-1918

New church at Yiewsley, 1859

By 1895 Yiewsley's population was nearly three thousand. The little church, seating only two hundred and eighty, was far too small to meet the needs of all the parishioners, so three mission rooms had been opened in outlying parts of the parish, that at Starveall continuing until 1926. There were four hundred Sunday School children and classes were held for a hundred and seventy older children who had left the Sunday School. In addition the church ran two Bands of Hope, three communicants' guilds, two temperance societies, two mission associations, four mothers' meetings, savings clubs and classes for canal workers. It was therefore decided to enlarge the church and the plans submitted by Mr. Nicholson of Beaumont Street, W. were accepted. The enlarged church was consecrated on April 25th 1898 by the Bishop of London and the whole cost of the work, £3782. 1s 9d (£3782.09) had been met by the end of 1899. Early in 1908 the Parish Room in Trout Road, which had been built by Messrs. Try & Hancock, was opened by the Bishop of Kensington.

Many Irish immigrants came to West Drayton after the Irish potato famine of the 1840's. They settled mainly in cottages which occupied the site of the present Daisy Villas on The Green. In some cases twenty or more people lived in one of these cottages which became known as the Irish hovels. The immigrants worked on the land, in the brickfields and on the construction of the branch railway line to Uxbridge. Most of them were *Roman Catholics* and their nearest place of worship was at North Hyde, between Hayes and Southall. Some of them would have walked there and back to attend mass each Sunday.

Later a priest would celebrate mass for them in a stable at the rear of the King's Head. By 1862 the Rev. Andrew Mooney was using a cottage in Money Lane as a school and was conducting services there. The Rev. Peter Elkins, who had succeeded him by 1867, wrote a letter to the local press addressed "to the Roman Catholics (if any) of Uxbridge and its vicinity" informing them that "West Drayton is erected into a mission" and inviting them to join over three hundred West Drayton Roman Catholics at Sunday Mass.

Shortly afterwards Father Elkins was succeeded by the Rev. Michael Wren who was to remain in West Drayton until his death on March 13th, 1896. Within a few weeks Father Wren had purchased a house and land from the executors of Mrs. Kearney for £855. The house (demolished in 1968) he used as his presbytery and the coach house and stables became a school and a temporary church. On September 29th, 1869 *St. Catherine's Church* was solemnly opened by Cardinal Manning. By then the congregation had risen to four hundred. In 1892 a mission church dedicated to Our Lady of Lourdes and St. Michael was opened in Lawn Road, Uxbridge.

Methodist meetings were held in the British School in 1853. The membership gradually increased and in 1871 steps were being taken to build a small chapel in Yiewsley High Street on a site given by Mr. and Mrs. Bridgett of Ealing Park. Donations came from as far away as Pinner and Rickmansworth and the building opened in December, 1872 with accommodation for a hundred and twenty. Like all the local churches of this period, the Methodists catered for a large number of children and young people, and in 1878 there were a hundred and twenty present at the Band of Hope tea.

Methodism flourished in the district and in 1913 there was talk of building a larger church, but this was delayed by the Great War. Efforts to raise the necessary funds started as soon as the war ended, but it was not until August 31st, 1927 that the Methodist Central Hall opened in Fairfield Road with the Rev. Maldwyn Edwards as its minister. The new church had seating for six hundred and the total cost of the building and the site was £18,000. The Central Hall remained the home of Yiewsley Methodists until 1973 when the present church and a supermarket were erected on its site.

The work of the *Salvation Army* in the district commenced in 1886 and its early "barracks" were in a building at Eastfield's brickfield and then in Thomas Clayton's large barn where as many as two hundred and fifty would attend the evening service. A site in Horton Road was bought in 1913 for £100 and by May the following year the present hall had been built by Mr. W. J. Wilkinson of West Drayton. Membership was then seventy-three adults and nearly two hundred children. The total cost of the building was £813 of which headquarters paid £300. When the hall was opened £458 of the balance had already been raised locally.

A congregation of the *Free Church of England*, known as *Emmanuel Church*, was started by the Rev. G. H. Jones, headmaster of Padcroft College, in 1877. The church flourished during his ministry but began to decline when he left in 1884, and it closed in 1891. *Elim Hall* opened in Wimpole Road in 1908 as an offshoot of a Gospel Hall held in the British School. It could seat a hundred and fifty and at one time there were seventy Sunday School children. The hall was destroyed by fire in 1967 after being empty for three years. *Yiewsley & West Drayton Brotherhood* started in 1912 with Methodist support. It met on Sundays in the Co-operative Hall from 3 to 4 p.m. and membership was open to both men and women. In December, 1932 the Brotherhood closed down for an indefinite period and never re-opened.

The De Burgh Era 1786-1918

LOCAL GOVERNMENT

In Tudor times Justices of the Peace were made responsible for the administration of local government, but many of their duties eventually passed to the Vestry, whose chief officers were the churchwardens and the overseers of the poor. With the growth of the population during the 19th century it became more economical for certain aspects of local government to be administered by a group of parishes instead of by a single parish, so some of the Vestry's powers were transferred to such bodies as the Board of Guardians, the Metropolitan Police and local sanitary authorities.

The churchwardens' duties were many and varied. They were (and still are) the chief lay officers of the parish church. In 1863 Daniel Mercer and James Thatcher, the churchwardens, paid the West Drayton policeman 10s 0d (50p) for attending to the fires in St. Martin's Church at night for three years. It is not clear if he did this in his spare time or while on duty.

Churchwardens also had many duties not connected with the parish church. On November 18th, 1805 Richard Dyche and Thomas Robinson paid 15s 0d (75p) "for printing 500 bills for a robbery" but unfortunately their records give no details of the crime. In an agricultural district such as West Drayton churchwardens would be concerned about damage to the crops, and anyone who caught a sparrow could claim a farthing ($\frac{1}{10}$p) from the parish funds. No fewer than seventy-six dozen sparrow heads were presented to the churchwardens, William Ratcliff and Richard Rook in 1793 and they duly paid out 19s 0d (95p) from their funds. Sheep worrying by dogs caused Richard Dyche and Thomas Robinson to send the cryer round the village in 1806 proclaiming that "all dogs be shutt up" for which he was paid 1s 0d (5p).

Vestry meetings were usually held in the Swan Inn, and on June 9th 1839 it was agreed that all books, papers and documents relating to the church and also parliamentary awards should be kept in the parish chest. At the same meeting "the propriety of a proper pound being maintained in this parish" was considered. The village pound (in which straying cattle and sheep were "impounded") is believed to have existed in Money Lane close to Napoleon Cottages. In 1909, however, West Drayton Parish Council was not certain if the pound belonged to the parish.

In January, 1880 the vestry rejected the proposal of the Norwood Water Co. to supply tapped water to the parish and it was not until 1906 that the Rickmansworth & Uxbridge Valley Water Co.'s plans for a pumping station in Horton Road were approved by Uxbridge Rural District Council. Main drainage was also opposed by the vestry in 1886, when it decided "it is not desirable for a united drainage scheme for the parish with the district of Yiewsley to be completed by the Rural Sanitary Authority." Further discussions on this matter took place and on March 17th 1887 it was stated that "a drainage scheme for the parish is wholly unnecessary." It was emphasised that such a scheme could not exist without any existing adequate water supply, for the lack of which the vestry was itself to blame by its decision in 1880! Discussions, however, continued and on May 19th, 1887 the vestry agreed" to confer and co-operate with the rural sanitary authority in protecting the interests of the ratepayers of the parish of West Drayton."

Under the Local Government Act of 1894 the civil duties of the vestry and the churchwardens were transferred to parish and district councils.

WEST DRAYTON AND DISTRICT
Early 19th. Century

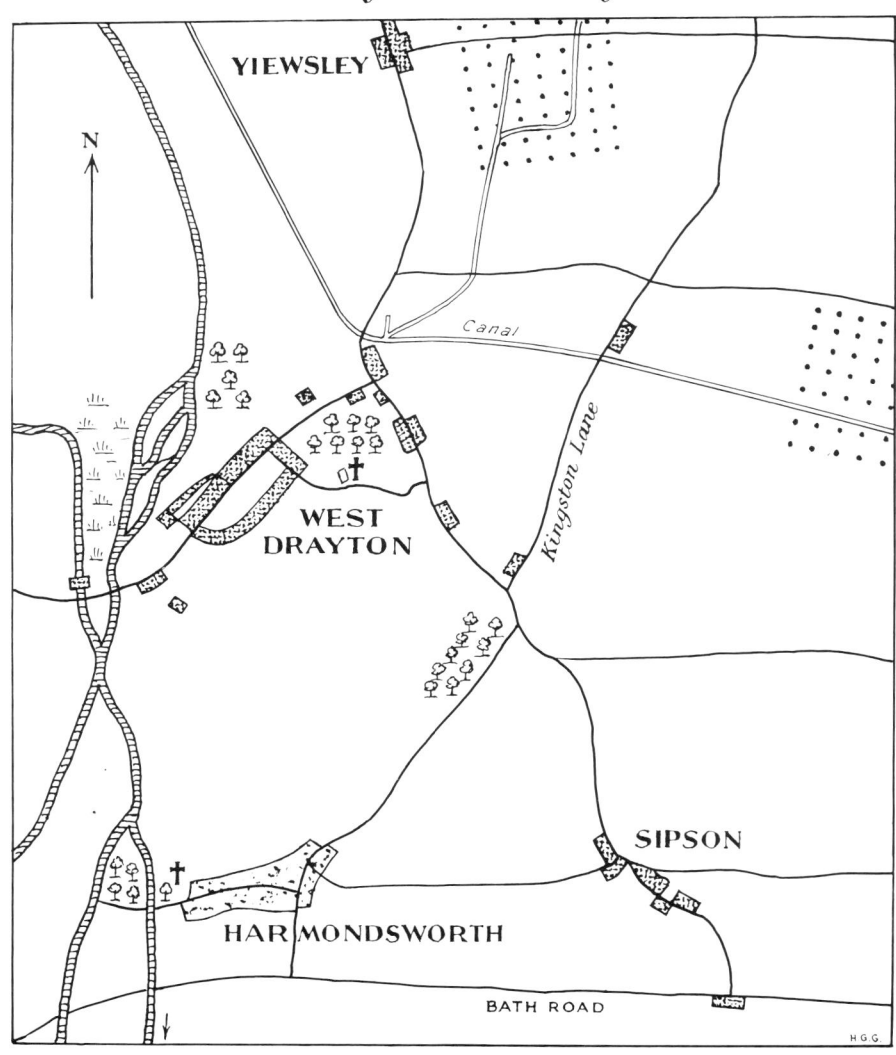

The De Burgh Era 1786-1918

WEST DRAYTON AND DISTRICT
1912

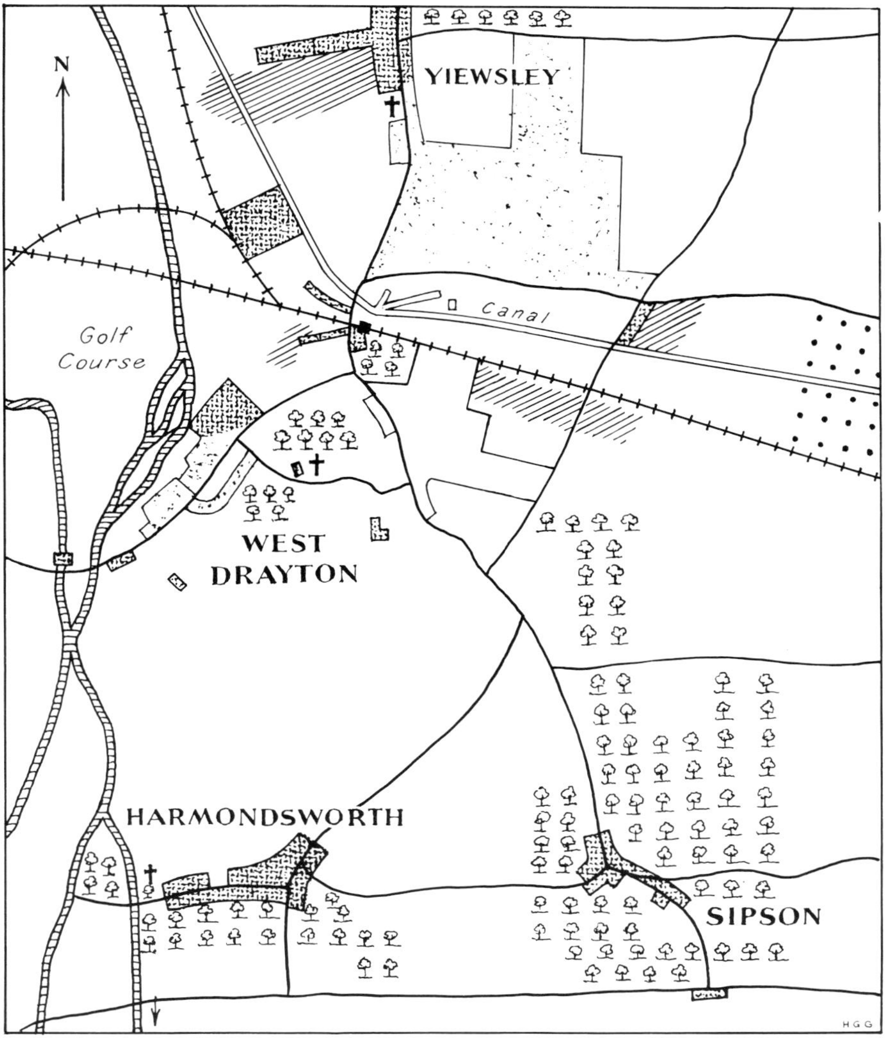

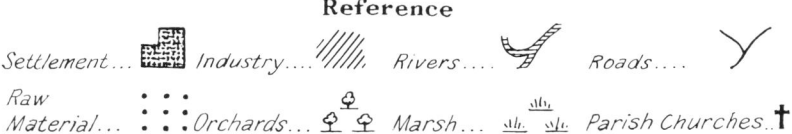

Reference

Settlement.... Industry.... Rivers.... Roads....
Raw Material... Orchards... Marsh... Parish Churches

West Drayton & Yiewsley through the centuries

Parish councils were elected at parish meetings, usually by a show of hands unless a poll was demanded. They had limited powers, and both West Drayton and Yiewsley also came under the jurisdiction of Uxbridge Rural District Council and the Middlesex County Council. It is hardly surprising, therefore, that there were occasions when the interests of the various authorities would clash. In 1896, Yiewsley, until then part of the civil parish of Hillingdon, was made a separate civil parish and early in the year both West Drayton and Yiewsley elected their first parish council.

The Otter Dock running from the canal to the brickfields had by then become derelict and a sanitary report in 1896 referred to the "abominable stench caused by a deposit of manure" which came from it. In 1907 Uxbridge Rural District Council made up Dock Road (now Colham Avenue) but drained the surface water into the derelict dock, thus causing a dispute with Yiewsley Parish Council who wished to drain the dock and fill it in. This and other disputes continued for many months. The work of filling in the dock eventually started in 1909 but was not completed until 1911. The Metropolitan Public Gardens Association gave seventy trees for planting on the reclaimed site, renamed Colham Avenue in 1938. The cost of acquiring the dock, filling it in and the tree planting was £272. 14s 0d (£272.70) of which Middlesex County Council paid £68. 3s 9d (£68.19).

In the early 20th century Uxbridge Rural District Council and the two parish councils were involved in making up roads in the district and on occasions West Drayton Parish Council would be opposed to the work as it would increase the rates. In 1904 there were still no street name plates in Yiewsley.

Street lighting was always debated by the parish councils and every effort was made to keep down costs. It was not until 1897 that Yiewsley Parish Council agreed to place seventeen gas lamps in the High Street, Horton Road and Trout Road and to employ a lamplighter at 5s 0d (25p) per week. The following year Robert Holmes, the lamplighter, threatened to resign as he had been asked to clean the lamps as well as light them. By then he was being paid 7s 0d (35p) a week and Mr. Foyer, the council chairman, suggested "they pay a little extra until they got the report of the Lighting Committee."

In 1896 West Drayton Parish Council erected three new gas lamps and ordered seven others at a cost of £2. 16s 6d (£2.82½) each. In a tape recorded interview the late Miss M. F. Ratcliff, who was a young girl at the time, recalled "The Council went round to find the spots where a light was needed and they found it was very difficult to find the entrance to Money Lane near St. Catherine's Church and the road leading from De Burgh Crescent to The Green (i.e. Church Road), and it was rather difficult to find the alley (Courting Alley) leading to Harmondsworth round what was our house. So they decided there must be a light there." But the siting of the other lamps caused some adverse comment for it was said "every councillor had arranged to have a light outside his own house to guide him home on foggy nights."

In 1910 Yiewsley was granted urban powers. The old parish council was replaced by Yiewsley Urban District Council which held its first meeting in May 1911 under the chairmanship of Mr. A. Saunders. The question of West Drayton becoming part of the new urban district was discussed at some length, but in October, 1916 West Drayton Parish Council was adamant that the "time was inexpedient to amalgamate with Yiewsley."

SOCIAL LIFE

After visiting the Great Exhibition in Hyde Park in 1851 a young local boy wrote in his diary "I visited the exhibition five times. Last time J. and I were there on the last shilling day. We were there from the opening until the exhibition closed at night. . . . Uncle Joe gave us in addition to the holiday each time 2s 6d (12½p) and some apples." Not all West Drayton boys at that time were as fortunate as young William Ratcliff in having such a kind and generous uncle. Indeed, for many of them a visit to Uxbridge Fair would have been the farthest they would have ventured from their own village.

During the 19th century, however, there was much to interest the people of West Drayton and Yiewsley in their own locality, for in those days people made their own entertainment and got a lot of pleasure out of it. Penny readings were very popular and these were held in the National School with the vicar, the Rev. Robert De Burgh, taking a prominent part. In 1865 and 1866 the Strollers Concert Party visited West Drayton and gave performances in aid of the National School funds. Among those taking part were Mr. Wallace Wells of the Royal Italian Opera and the Brothers Seymour from New York. We are told that these concerts were patronised by "the elite of the neighbourhood."

The schools were the only places available for social gatherings and so served a dual purpose. At a concert held in the British School in 1881 "the performance of Miss Emma Belch on the harmonium was somewhat marred by the inefficiency of the instrument." Many local societies had been formed at this period and by 1886 Yiewsley Choral Society, West Drayton String Band, Yiewsley & West Drayton Drum & Fife Band (conductor Mr. Whatley, headmaster of the British School), Yiewsley Minstrel Troupe and West Drayton Dramatic Society were functioning. Yiewsley & West Drayton Silver Band was formed in 1890 with Mr. H. Chandler as its Hon. Secretary. Over ninety years later the band was still very active and the name Chandler appeared in its list of officers.

In the early 20th century came the West Drayton Musical Society (conductor William Ratcliff) which gave a concert for the Belgian refugees in December, 1914. Annual pantomimes produced by Mr. & Mrs. Walker of The Grange, West Drayton were very popular for many years as were the performances of the West Drayton Mummers. Mr. Strickland of 7, De Burgh Crescent was much in demand at Sunday School treats, for he possessed a gramophone.

The first cinema came in 1911 when the People's Electric Theatre opened in Station Road on January 28th. It had 360 tip-up seats and also "a nice and convenient lounge on the same principle as the latest style of London theatres." The cinema generated its own electricity and proposed to supply the adjacent Railway Hotel. In June, 1911 a film of George V's coronation was screened and a year later some people were paying five or six visits a week to the cinema. Opposition, however, came with the opening of the Marlborough Cinema, Yiewsley in 1923 and the People's Electric Theatre eventually closed. The building later became Pat's Garage and in 1982 an open air market was held on its site.

There were plenty of outdoor activities. Event such as jubilees and coronations were the occasion for much local festivity. The Green was the venue for celebrations on May Day and Empire Day and also the scene for the Guy Fawkes Night bonfire. West Drayton Fair was held there every Whit Monday until it was abolished in 1880 under the Fairs Act of 1871 as "it would be for the

West Drayton & Yiewsley through the centuries

Empire Day, 1913

convenience and advantage of the public that such a fair should be abolished."

Hunting was popular and was supported by Hubert De Burgh and his brother, the vicar. In 1863 the landlord of the De Burgh Arms offered accommodation to those who hunted with the Queen's Stag Hounds, the Prince's Harriers and Lord Lonsdale's Hounds. The Greenford Draghounds passed through West Drayton in March 1894 with a good muster of huntsmen. Stags were brought into the district for hunting. In January, 1914 the Berks. & Bucks. Stag Hounds started a hunt from Uxbridge Moor. The stag was chased through Richardson's Farm, Yiewsley and then into White's Farm. The hunt continued through Miss Butler's garden, down the High Street to the Red Cow. The stag continued its flight through Colham Green to Hayes, where it was impaled on an iron fence and killed.

West Drayton Cricket Club existed by the early 1870's and had strong support from the Rev. Robert De Burgh. In its early days matches were played on various pitches — in the grounds of Drayton House and Dog Kennel Meadow (where West Drayton Primary School now stands) — and on its present ground since the 1880's. There was an outstanding bowling performance in May, 1894 when George Thornhill took seven wickets in six overs without a run being scored. On September 2nd, 1902 C. Aubrey Smith, who then lived at Avenue House, was elected a member. West Drayton could then claim to have a Test cricketer in its side, for Aubrey Smith had captained England in the first Test Match played in South Africa in 1888.

There were many football clubs in West Drayton and Yiewsley towards the end of the 19th century, the foremost being Yiewsley F.C. In 1902 the

The De Burgh Era 1786-1918

club combined with Yiewsley Rovers F.C., which then became the reserve side. The club still continues, although in another form, as Hillingdon Borough F.C.

During the 1860's and 1870's West Drayton Race Course brought much notoriety to the village. It occupied the site of the Garden City, covering an area of over 42 acres, and was let to George French of Bedford Cottage, Trout Lane (who preferred to be known as Count Bolo) at a rent of £200 per annum. The races attracted many undesirables from London, an estimated ten thousand attending the Whitsun Meeting in 1873. After these meetings Uxbridge Police Court was kept busy with robbery and assault cases. On July 17th, 1874 *The Times* published a letter from an American visitor who complained "I saw nothing there in the least degree worthy of the name of sport.... You will scarce believe it when I tell you, Sir, that a large proportion of the gentlemen with whom I came into contact were nothing but blackguards.... A certain number of the people engaged in furthering the interest of good horse breeding at West Drayton were, I should say, likewise engaged in looking for something to turn up at the end of a carelessly guarded watch chain."

French was declared bankrupt in 1876 and in September, 1877 the grandstand at the race course, which was insured for £2,000, was destroyed in a mysterious fire just two days before the fire insurance policy expired. The insurance company was suspicious about the whole affair and would not pay cash compensation, but offered to rebuild the stand instead. The course was eventually closed under the Metropolitan Racecourse Act of 1879. George French died on April 4th, 1878 at Bedford Cottage in very reduced circumstances. It was said that he possessed a number of warm-hearted friends but that his worst enemy was himself.

The Board Mill after the fire, 1913

West Drayton Golf Club opened in 1895. This was an eighteen hole course on an eighty acre site which included part of the old race course and extended to the rear of West Drayton Mill. Its membership consisted mainly of London business men who paid an annual subscription of three guineas. The former Colham Mill House (which still stands at the entrance to the Garden City) became the club house and comprised dressing rooms, luncheon rooms and a smoking room as well as accommodation for caddies and club servants. The club flourished until the Great War, which caused a drop in its membership and its eventual closure.

On bank holidays and other occasions when there were no race meetings the race course was used for other gatherings. Greyhound coursing followed by dinner in the De Burgh Arms was popular in the 1870's and had the blessing of the vicar, the Rev. Robert De Burgh, but was opposed by the R.S.P.C.A. Fetes which attracted many hundreds of outsiders often resulted in behaviour which was deplored by local residents. In September, 1877 an ox and a sheep were roasted whole and the visitors allowed to help themselves. The scene was described as disgusting and revolting. People rushed to the carcases like wolves or savages and cut, slashed and tore them to pieces. "One daughter of Eve reduced to the last extreme for a wrapper was seen to utilise one of her petticoats."

Despite scenes like this, however, most people who went to these fetes would have enjoyed themselves. Some three thousand are believed to have visited the August Bank Holiday Fete in 1875, but for two of them it seems to have ended on a sad note. In the "agony column" of the local paper for August 7th, 1875 appears the following:

"ANNIE — Perhaps your memory fails you. When returning in a Fly from Drayton Fete to Uxbridge your promise was to Meet me on Wednesday last, which you did not. I want to see you again, so meet me same time and place and I will explain all. GEORGE"

THE GREAT WAR

"The war absorbs all our thoughts. We feel it to be a just one in so far as England is concerned." So wrote the Rev. A. W. S. A. Row in his parish magazine in September, 1914. The war was to prove a worrying time for many in West Drayton, including the Vicar, whose son was serving as an army captain. Many local men served in the forces either as volunteers or as conscripts. One young lad, Charlie Hancock, managed to enlist although under age. He came home blind, but lived a long and cheerful life until his death in 1981. Within two months of the outbreak of hostilities, twenty-one Stockley men had volunteered and by 1916 Albert Road had seventy-one of its men serving in the forces. Altogether Yiewsley provided five hundred and thirty men for the army or navy.

In the early months troops guarded the railway line as a precaution against sabotage and the 2nd King Edward's Horse and a naval brigade held manoeuvres in the district. A Yiewsley & West Drayton Volunteer Force was set up and also the West Drayton Voluntary Helpers who provided comforts for the fighting men. The Yiewsley baker, Mr. F. Clinch, sent cakes to local men serving with the forces and received a letter of thanks from Rifleman W. Littleworth which concluded "I have met a lot of chaps from Yiewsley who you know — young Bateman and Mr. Tom Hancock's son Bill."

The district did not suffer air raids as in the Second World War, but precautions were taken. A searchlight unit was established in West Drayton and in May, 1915 two aeroplanes were caught in its beams. At first it was thought that a Zeppelin raid was imminent until it was realised that the aircraft were not hostile. In 1916 the churchwardens at St. Martin's Church thought it advisable to insure the church against damage by aerial attack and put out a special appeal to meet the cost of the annual premium of four guineas. St. Martin's had already experienced some of the problems caused by the war when Mr. Bulland, its organist, left in December, 1915 to enlist in the Artists' Rifles.

Belgian refugees were housed in the district and a fund was set up to assist them. When a German threat to Paris seemed possible Mrs. Hubbard evacuated her girls' school from the French capital to the safety of Drayton Hall. A tribunal was set up under the chairmanship of the Rev. F. D. Sturgess, Vicar of Yiewsley, to consider applications for call-up exemptions. With the growing U-boat menace the need for home food production increased, and West Drayton Parish Council made strenuous efforts to obtain land for use as allotments.

Fund raising was much in evidence. During Red Cross week in 1918 West Drayton collected £22. 8s 3d (£22.42) and Yiewsley £80. 3s 1d (£80.15½) of which £31. 13s 8d (£31.67) came from a war relics exhibition and tea. In January, 1917 West Drayton School Savings Association was formed and by the end of the war its 221 members had subscribed £1005.

Armistice Day, November 11th 1918, saw great rejoicing throughout the district. Detonators were set off on the railway line, factories and schools closed, flags appeared everywhere and a special mass was celebrated in St. Catherine's Church. One hundred and twenty Yiewsley men died in the war, and eleven from Stockley. At West Drayton, forty-one dead are commemorated on the war memorial in St. Martin's Church and their names are read at the Remembrance Day service each year.

West Drayton & Yiewsley through the centuries

Top: The Swan Inn   Bottom: The old blacksmith's shop, 1923

Chapter Five

Armistice and Second War 1918 – 1945

THE AFTERMATH OF THE GREAT WAR
The men returning from the war received a warm welcome from their relatives and neighbours and in 1919 were given a "welcome home" party in West Drayton National School, while at Yiewsley there was a dinner and smoking concert in the Church Room. But the "land fit for heroes" promised by the politicians failed to materialise. There were employment and housing problems on a large scale and some of the demobbed service men decided to emigrate.

One who did so was John Parker, who was born at 67, Mill Road in 1888 and later lived at 4, Tyrrell's Cottages in Horton Lane (now demolished). After serving in the forces during the war, he married, but was unable to find a house in the district, so in 1920 he emigrated to Canada. Sixty years later he flew into Heathrow Airport by jumbo jet to revisit the scenes of his youth. He was then in his ninety-second year and very active both mentally and physically. In a tape-recorded interview he recalled the district as he remembered it in his boyhood and found it had "wonderfully improved." The greatest change was in the roads, many of which were only "cow paths" sixty years before. He died a few weeks after flying home to Toronto.

Peace celebrations were held in both villages in the summer of 1919, although that at Yiewsley did not have the official blessing of the local council, which declined to give its support "until we are at peace with all nations." Various suggestions were discussed as to the provision of war memorials. At West Drayton a parish meeting agreed to have a rough-hewn block of granite outside St. Martin's Church, but an appeal for £300 to meet the cost of this failed to reach the target. Two other suggestions were then rejected — a lych gate at the church as being impracticable, and a cross in the churchyard which could meet with objections. Finally it was agreed to place a memorial in the church. Similar problems occurred in the erection of the Yiewsley war memorial. Eventually three memorials were unveiled in the district in 1921 — at Stockley in January, at Yiewsley in June and at West Drayton in July.

HOUSING
Housing proved to be a big problem in the years between the wars, as indeed it is today. In 1920 parts of the living quarters at West Drayton Royal Air Force Station, which had earlier been occupied by the Royal Naval Air Service, were empty, and both Yiewsley Urban District Council and Uxbridge Rural District Council were anxious that the buildings should be used for civilian housing purposes. In the House of Commons a Labour M.P., Mr. F. Hall, suggested that demobbed service men might be housed there, but the Secretary of State for War

and Air (Mr. Winston Churchill) replied that after careful consideration it had been decided that it was not possible "to admit the demobilised as resident people over whom the ministry had no control."

The first *council houses* were built in the 1920's. Early in 1921 Uxbridge Rural District Council bought a 3¼ acre field known as Mill Close (and with it the obligation to pay the Trustees of the West Drayton Parochial Charities £1 annually) for development as the *St. Martin's Road Council Estate*. Yiewsley Urban District Council's scheme for the *Whitethorn Avenue Estate* of 120 houses was already under way and by August 1921 8 houses and 12 flats had been completed. Tenders for a further 50 houses costing £431 each were accepted in February 1922 and the work was finished by March 1923 when 16 flats and 242 houses had been built. In April the weekly rents were reduced from 11s 0d (55p) to 10s 5d (52½p) for flats, 12s 3d (c. 61p) to 11s 6d (57½p) for non-parlour type houses, 13s 6d (67½p) to 13s 0d (65p) for the parlour type and from 16s 6d (82½p) to 16s 0d (80p) for the larger houses.

Other council developments soon followed. In 1925 Yiewsley Urban District Council accepted the tender of A. C. Dean of High Wycombe amounting to £27,000 for building 52 houses and in 1928 that of Messrs. C. Mishen & Sons, St. Albans of £103,578 for 246 houses in the Falling Lane area plus a further £14,900 for roads and sewers. This development involved the demolition of an old house known as "The Castle" which gave its name to Castle Avenue.

A vast slum clearance scheme brought further council housing estates in the 1930's. The layout of *Bell Farm Estate* was approved in 1937 and tenders for 120 houses considered. The following year it was decided to build a further 200 houses on this estate. By the end of 1938 136 houses had been built and tenders were invited for a further 204. Then came the Second World War, which delayed the completion of this estate until the 1950's. The first local authority sheltered accommodation was erected in 1934 in Providence Road.

In addition to the Local Authority housing schemes there was also much private development between the wars. First came *West Drayton Garden City*, which in spite of its name lay within Yiewsley parish. This occupied the site of the old race course and part of the golf course, a fact which is recalled in the name of one of its roads, Fairway Avenue. On this estate plots could be purchased for £80 to £100 and the cost of erecting a small bungalow would be in the region of £250. A six-roomed house could be built for £450. Many of the plots were sufficiently large to allow for the construction of a tennis court. In later years this led to much in-filling on the estate as many of these large gardens were sold for building.

The developer's brochure stated that the estate was "a grand retreat for jaded city workers" and that the season ticket rate at Paddington was less than 6d (2½p) per day. Water, electricity and gas were laid on but no mention was made of main drainage. Indeed, this did not come until some years later, and in its early days sewage disposal on the Garden City was by means of cesspits. As the estate extended, not everybody was able to have main water immediately, and in 1927 sixty-seven owners asked the Rickmansworth & Uxbridge Valley Water Co. to extend its supply to their part of the Estate.

The brochure stated that "the Estate was used as a golf course and owing to its magnificent bed of ballast subsoil the course was always dry, even during the wettest season." But this statement could have been of little comfort to the residents when the river overflowed its banks to a depth of several feet in 1936.

Armistice and Second War 1918-1945

The Garden City roads were made up at the end of 1935 and the owners of the larger plots, especially those on corner sites, were faced with heavy costs. One astute owner is said to have solved his problem in a very novel way. He is stated to have had the whole of his frontage, excepting the gateway, legally conveyed to a tramp to a depth of two or three feet. The tramp, duly rewarded, continued his travels and the owner was thus only legally liable for road charges on his drive entrance.

Early in 1923 *Drayton House* was offered for sale by auction and sold to Mr. H. H. Pearce for £9,000. The estate was over 18 acres in extent and consisted of the land bounded by Swan Road, Station Road, Old Farm Road and the river. The purchase price also included another 3 acres on the eastern side of Swan Road. The fine old house was then demolished and its ornamental wrought iron entrance gates sold to Mr. Penrose, who re-erected them at Oxhey Grange, Bushey, near Watford. A new road, Ferrers Avenue (named after a former owner of the estate, Lord Ferrers) was then constructed through the centre of the estate.

The land was divided into plots which had a minimum frontage of 25ft and depths varying from 150ft to 400ft. Prices ranged from £4 to £6. 10s 0d (£6.50) per foot frontage according to position and depth. Land fronting Station Road was reserved for shops and was offered at £8 per foot frontage.

Part of the Station Road frontage was sold to the Post Office in 1928, but it was not until 1932 that work was started on clearing the site. The new post office opened in June 1933 and the sub-post office forming part of Mrs. Gray's shop at 15, The Green then closed. A new sub-post office for Yiewsley was then opened in Platt's Stores in the High Street. This took the place of Yiewsley Post Office which was next to the Red Cow. These premises were then taken over by Mr. R. H. Smith, a local butcher.

Plans were then passed for a new automatic telephone exchange next to the new West Drayton Post Office. It opened in 1938 when the exchange was renamed West Drayton. Earlier, while housed at 87, Station Road, the exchange had been known as Yiewsley.

A small bungalow development of about 2 acres was started in 1928 on land next to the parish church and named *Bagley Close* after the Bagley family who farmed in West Drayton in the 19th century. This development was opposed by West Drayton Parish Council as "in the opinion of the Council the erection of bungalows on this land would be detrimental to the neighbouring properties and to the amenities of the parish." In an attempt to stop the development the Parish Council considered acquiring the land as a cemetery under the Burial Act of 1853 but it had acted far too late. Uxbridge Rural District Council passed the plans and the developer, Captain A. S. Adams, a Canadian, of The Alders, Denham Road, Uxbridge, built the bungalows. They were offered for sale at £625 and £650 for the two bedroom type and £725 for those with three bedrooms. Repayments on a twenty year mortgage worked out at just under £1 per week and rates at less than 5s 0d (25p). Bagley Close was built on the site of the kitchen garden of Lord Paget's Manor House. Most of the surrounding high Tudor brick wall was demolished and provided sufficient bricks to build five of the bungalows in Bagley Close and also a semi-bungalow in Church Road.

Shortly after Bagley Close was completed Messrs. C. E. Langer & Co. began developing the Bagley Garden Estate, which was soon renamed *Drayton Gardens*. They claimed that "these wonderfully charming homes are surely the most remarkable value ever offered in house property." Intending

West Drayton & Yiewsley through the centuries

purchasers had the choice of four types of houses, the prices being £650, £795, £830 and £850. Deposits on a twenty year mortgage were as little as £25, with the repayments working out at 21s 0d (£1.05) a week plus 3s 9d (19p) a week for rates.

A little while later came *Cherry Orchard*, a name which describes the previous use of the land. Another estate of small houses was also being erected in the Sipson Road by the Napier Development Co. At first it was known as Napier Road but in 1937 it was renamed Thornton Avenue.

The final large-scale private development of the inter-war years was *West Drayton Park Avenue*, an estate of good class houses built in a large field next to Drayton Hall. Later, in 1966 it was extended and the new houses were advertised "from £6950." Although West Drayton Park Avenue marked the end of large-scale private development until after the end of the Second World War, houses were built on various small plots of land throughout the district.

EMPLOYMENT

Unemployment was a big problem for the district in the years between the wars, especially during the 1930's. The cause for this was both national and local. The demobilised servicemen flooded the labour market nationwide and this caused wages to be low.

In 1926 came the General Strike, lasting over a week. Yiewsley Urban District Council immediately formed an emergency committee to deal with the control of food and fuel resources. Only one train was in operation to serve the two branch lines to Uxbridge and Staines. The Ivy Leaf Club in Yiewsley opened its premises to both unemployed and strikers for recreational purposes, and a strike meeting held in the Co-operative Hall was so overcrowded that many had to be turned away. Two hundred and fifty people attended a special service in St. Matthew's Church at which the Vicar, the Rev. J. S. L. Jones, was joined by the Baptist Minister, the Rev. Matthew Flint — an amazing event in those days, for the ecumenical movement locally was still at least three decades away.

There was a significant change in the type of employment. The brickfields were nearly worked out and much of the agricultural land was being sold for building purposes. Industry was moving into the district and this resulted in the building of factories, perhaps the most important of which was the Anglo-Swiss Screw Co. founded by Oscar Frey in 1919. Factory work could also be found in neighbouring towns such as Uxbridge, Hayes, Slough and Staines.

The private housing estate developments were bringing another type of worker into West Drayton — the commuter. There was easy access to West Drayton by train, and many who worked in London but wished to live in rural surroundings were attracted into the district by the estate developers' brochures.

TRANSPORT

For those working outside West Drayton some form of transport was essential. Hayes, Uxbridge, Slough and Staines were within easy cycling distance, while those who could afford it might make the journey by motor cycle or car.

The railway provided a fast and efficient service to Paddington, some non-stop trains doing the journey in eighteen minutes. In 1931 West Drayton Station was served by a hundred and twelve trains each weekday. Forty-two of these went to Paddington, fifty to Uxbridge and twenty to Staines. The third class monthly season ticket to Paddington was £1. 7s 9d (£1.39) and the day return ticket to Uxbridge was 4d (2p).

Armistice and Second War 1918-1945

The old railway bridge, demolished in 1960

During the early 1930's the 501 and 506 bus routes provided 29 buses each way to Uxbridge on a weekday, the journey taking 17 minutes. There were also fifteen No. 501 buses to and from Hounslow (a 23 minute journey), while the 506 bus made fourteen journeys in each direction to Staines (53 minutes).

The increase in motor traffic stressed the need for wider roads. Early in 1939 work commenced on widening Station Road and rebuilding the canal bridge. It was indeed fortunate that the work started early in the year. Had it been delayed for a few months the whole scheme would have been held up for many years owing to the outbreak of war.

SCHOOLS

The increasing population of the district caused by the new housing estates presented a problem for the local schools. Some of the buildings were nearly a century old and the need for their expansion and modernisation was urgent.

In 1923 *West Drayton National School* had a staff of six and a roll of 211 pupils. It was perhaps fortunate that the average attendance amounted to 178, for the school only had accommodation for 198. In 1926 John Turner (known to his pupils as "Gaffer") retired as headmaster after 28 years' service and was succeeded by Mr. W. R. F. Smart. The Middlesex County Council's plan to widen Station Road meant that the school would lose most of its playground and also the

West Drayton & Yiewsley through the centuries

school house which was then being used for classes. The decision was taken, therefore, to build a new church school in Kingston Lane at the rear of the Vicarage, but negotiations with the county council over compensation to be paid for the land to be taken for road widening were prolonged. Work started on the road widening early in 1939, but all thoughts of building the new school in the immediate future had to be abandoned when war came in September. The school continued in the old building but without its playground and the school house. Other problems then arose. When the school re-opened after the summer holidays in 1946 two classes were housed in a hut in the school yard and the remaining three classes met in the recently opened Cherry Lane School, as the old school building was considered unsafe and the sanitary conditions were bad. The school governors then agreed to its closure, but discussions were resumed on the building of a new church school.

St. Catherine's School was also having accommodation problems. In 1923 there were two teachers and a roll of sixty pupils with accommodation for twelve more. The buildings, however, were inadequate and the number of pupils began to increase. In 1930 Mr. S. A. J. McVeigh became headmaster and remained for nearly twenty years. During his headmastership the decision was taken to build a new school, and plans for this were submitted in 1937. The school was built two years later with places for 240 pupils. Children of all ages up to fifteen were admitted, but later the school was changed to primary status.

St. Matthew's School was the largest of the church schools. It had a staff of eight in 1923 with a roll of 387 pupils and accommodation for 405. Like the other church schools St. Matthew's had financial problems, and in 1920 parents were asked to subscribe towards some much-needed repairs. Charles Heron, a strict and much respected headmaster, retired in 1924 after thirty-two years. He could recall the days when Yiewsley had a population of about a thousand, when there was no gas or drainage and only four shops.

Another long service teacher, Mrs. Turner, retired as headmistress of *West Drayton Primary School* in 1921, having held the post since the school opened in 1905. The school could accommodate 150 pupils, but in 1923 there were only 120 names on the roll and a staff of three. The rapid development of the district is reflected in the fact that by 1937 the staff numbered ten and two years later the school was so overcrowded that an additional class had to be accommodated in the Baptist Church until a hut could be erected in the playground to house fifty pupils. At the outbreak of war in September, 1939 the pupils were sent home as the building was taken over as an A.R.P. Centre. Voluntary classes were started in the hut in October and home groups were inaugurated during November. It was not until January, 1940 that the school could resume in the main building, after the A.R.P. first aid unit had transferred to the hut.

Two Yiewsley schools which no longer exist, *Providence Road* and *St. Stephen's*, each had a staff of six in 1923. St. Stephen's was the larger with space for 310 and a roll of 288 against Providence Road's 288 places and 257 pupils.

A new school opened in the Yiewsley area on March 11th, 1936. This was *Evelyns*, which took its name from a private school that had been founded in 1872 by Mr. G. T. Worsley. The Middlesex Schools Gazette described it as "an educational palace." The first headmaster was Mr. R. L. Bidgood, who later transferred to West Drayton Primary School. Evelyns had accommodation for

Armistice and Second War 1918-1945

440 senior boys and a similar number of senior girls. It was built by Mr. W. S. Try of Cowley at a cost of £32,000.

A problem that faced the education authorities was providing for the children who lived on barges moving along the canal. In 1930 the Grand Union Canal Co. provided a *Floating School* for these children in the barge "Elsdale" which was anchored on the canal at Yiewsley. It was estimated that about a hundred children would use the school (which had accommodation for forty) during the course of a week. The Floating School remained at Yiewsley until 1939 when it was moved to Bulls Bridge, Southall.

In 1931 the local estate agents, Messrs. John J. Southall & Co., leased "The Copse" on West Drayton Green to Miss H. W. White and Miss L. G. Butler for use as a private school, which they named "Heathlands." This school catered for both day and boarding pupils and provided education from kindergarten to the age of sixteen. The lease must have been short, for within a year or two the school had moved to less pleasant premises in De Burgh Crescent, where it continued to exist for a few years.

Until 1939 there were several music teachers throughout West Drayton and Yiewsley who received pupils in their homes. Perhaps the best known of these was Mr. A. F. Johns of 68, Swan Road. His prospectus showed that he taught piano, mandoline, violin, viola, 'cello, guitar, banjo, flute, piccolo, voice production, etc. The fees ranged from £1. 1s 0d (£1.05) to £3. 3s 0d (£3.15) a

The Floating School, Yiewsley

term of thirteen lessons. Mr. Johns also received pupils for general educational subjects at his house, which at one time he called West Drayton Preparatory School.

THE CHURCHES

Most of the churches faced financial problems during the years of the depression in the 1930's. It was a particularly difficult period financially for *St. Martin's*, for it was faced with costly restoration work to its ancient fabric. In 1926 the tower was covered in ivy which had eaten into the stonework, making it unsafe in places. An estimate amounting to £1175 for removing the ivy and repairing the tower was accepted, and at the same time a brave attempt was made to raise a further £425 to recast and rehang the peal of bells, which had been removed when the wooden bell frame became unsafe. The tower was restored but it was not until 1931 that the debt had been paid. By 1932 sufficient money had been raised to fix a steel bell frame and to recast and rehang the tenor bell. Fifty years later, the remaining five bells still awaited sufficient funds to enable them to be returned to the belfry.

In 1931 the rest of the church was restored by Messrs. W. S. Try, Ltd. of Cowley at an estimated cost of £1600. The architects for this restoration were T. Gordon Jackson and a local architect, Hubert F. Bateman of Warwick Road. During the restoration electric lighting was installed in place of the gas lamps, the cost of this being paid by the Patron of the living, Miss Eva De Burgh.

In 1928 the Rev. A. W. S. A. Row retired as Vicar after a ministry lasting nearly thirty-nine years. He was succeeded by the Rev. Leslie E. Prout whose incumbency was to include the difficult days of the Second World War and its aftermath.

A few years before the Great War *West Drayton Baptists* had begun to think of building a new church to replace their old chapel in Money Lane where they had worshipped since 1827. The war, however, caused a postponement of their plans but in July, 1920 they held a garden party to raise money for the building fund. By the end of the year they had £400 in hand, which they considered was sufficient to buy and fence a plot of land in Station Road nearly opposite Brandville Road. In the end, however, they did not proceed with this scheme.

When Drayton House Estate was sold in 1923 the Baptists acquired a site on the east side of Swan Road and there they built their new church. The foundation stone of the school room was laid on July 9th, 1924 and the room was in use by October. The church was completed by the following March. It was built by a local builder, Samuel Bateman, to the design of his son, Hubert, at a cost of just over £3,000. It was in the new church that the Baptists celebrated their centenary on July 6th, 1927, when the proceedings opened with a parade by members of the church dressed in costumes of the period of 1827.

Yiewsley Baptists also considered building new premises. Reuben Smith, who had given the site of the Baptist Tabernacle in 1898, died in 1918 and left the church two adjoining houses for use as a manse and also £1,000. In 1934 this sum was used towards the cost of building new Sunday School accommodation at the other end of Colham Avenue, the foundation stones of which were laid in July. The total cost of the land and the building was £2775 and a further £175 was spent on furnishings. A member of the church, W. T. Morgan, gave his services free as architect. The schoolroom now forms part of the present Yiewsley Baptist Church complex.

After the war it was possible to start on certain improvements which were needed at *St. Matthew's Church*. The organ was presenting many problems and the Vicar, the Rev. F. D. Sturgess, commented that "sometimes it croaked at the beginning of services and sighed throughout the sermon," so in 1919 a fund was opened to provide a new organ, and Harry Richardson, who was a churchwarden at St. Matthew's for twenty-five years, donated £100 towards it. In 1924 the church accounts showed a deficit of £1. 0s. 5d (£1.02), mainly due to the fact that electric lighting had been installed at a cost of £86. 5s 6d (£86.27½). The deficit would have been considerably more had the church not received a legacy of £100 during the year from a former vicar, the Rev. H. Francis.

In 1937 the Rev. J. S. L. Jones, who had been vicar since 1921, retired owing to ill health and was succeeded by the Rev. F. W. Ruffle, who was to remain until 1973. The new vicar had to find temporary accommodation in St. Stephen's Road, for the old vicarage was being demolished. A new vicarage was built on part of the site and the remainder of the land was sold for development as a shopping parade.

In 1927 *Yiewsley Methodists* moved from their small chapel in the High Street to their new Central Hall, which had been built on the site of Golden Row cottages in Fairfield Road. The move from a very small chapel to a huge hall seating six hundred was an ambitious one but it was believed at the time that a large new building would be needed to meet the spiritual needs of the rapidly increasing population of the district.

The Central Hall not only provided the Methodists with a church but was often the venue for events such as concerts by the Yiewsley & West Drayton

The Central Hall, Yiewsley

West Drayton & Yiewsley through the centuries

Silver Band. During the ministry of the Rev. A. William Hopkins in the 1930's there were packed meetings of the Men's Fellowship when speakers such as the Rev. Dick Sheppard, Hannen Swaffer and Dr. Hewlett Johnson, the "Red" Dean of Canterbury, spoke on problems of national importance.

West Drayton & Yiewsley Congregational Church was formed in the mid-1920's, when services conducted by students from Hampstead College were held in the Co-operative Hall at 11 a.m. and 6.30 p.m. on Sundays. The Chairman of the church was Mr. T. Hancock of Otterfield Road, the Secretary and Sunday School Superintendent was Mr. J. Gwilt of Bellclose Road, and Mr. F. Crowther of Station Road acted as Treasurer. Some two hundred people were present at a social in January, 1925 in aid of the building fund, and it was proposed to build a church in the newly-constructed Ferrers Avenue. There was an outing to Burnham Beeches later in the year and a Sunday School party just after Christmas. The proposed church was never built and no further records of the Congregationalists have been traced. It is possible that they realised that the need for another church no longer existed with the opening of the Methodist Central Hall in 1927.

LOCAL GOVERNMENT

In 1919 West Drayton was still governed at local level by the parish council, which spent much of its time discussing lighting problems. It advertised for a part-time lamplighter at a wage of £1 a week but received no applications. In 1923 it fixed the lighting rate at 3d (c. 1½p) in the pound. The streets were then lit only during the winter months, and the lamps would be removed in the summer to avoid damage by vandals. In April, 1927 the Parish Council referred to the Lighting Committee Mr. H. Wilkinson's estimate for taking down the lanterns, storing and refixing them.

During the war and its immediate aftermath the council made strenuous efforts to obtain allotment land for West Drayton. Early in 1918 it was negotiating for the use of part of The Closes. Residents in Church Road opposed this, but by April 1919 fifty-four allotments were in use on the site. Opposition was then voiced by Mrs. Barnard, who had lived at the Gate House in the early years of the century but had moved from West Drayton before the war. The Vicar, the Rev. A. W. S. A. Row, however, strongly supported the action of the Parish Council in providing allotments for his parishioners, especially those who had served with the forces and were now unemployed.

In July, 1920 the Parish Council was negotiating for the use of seventeen acres of land in Harmondsworth Road for further much-needed allotment sites and hoped to have them in use by September. But nothing had happened six months later, as the Middlesex County Council had failed to reply to any letters. The matter dragged on another eight months, and then the Parish Council decided not to continue discussions as the rent being asked was considered excessive.

Early in 1921 the council wished to buy The Avenue (the tree-lined pathway from Church Road through The Closes) for use as an open space, and made an offer of £100. This was not accepted, but negotiations continued and eventually a parish meeting in 1924 agreed to a purchase price of £500. Two years later the Parish Council approached the County Council with regard to purchasing the rest of The Closes, then occupied by Mr. Edward Lovejoy as grazing land. Again the negotiations were protracted and anxiety was felt when it

The old Anchor Public House and blacksmith's shop which were demolished during the rebuilding of Colham Bridge in 1939

became known that Middlesex County Council had thoughts of selling the land to a private builder. Finally, in December 1926, agreement was reached and the County Council agreed to sell the land for £3,000.

Meanwhile, Yiewsley Urban District Council was also active in obtaining land for recreational purposes. In 1926 it announced its intention to provide a recreation ground on part of Rabbs Farm and to buy Clark's Meadows. In 1928 a bandstand accommodating thirty players was erected in Yiewsley Recreation Ground at a cost of £300 and four hard tennis courts were in use.

One of the last problems dealt with by West Drayton Parish Council was the naming of Swan Road. Various other names were then being given to it. The Drayton House Estate brochure referred to it as Mill Road, while a picture postcard even called it Station Road. A letter from Uxbridge Rural District Council about this matter was discussed by the Parish Council on February 28th 1928, when "it was resolved to inform the Rural Council it is desired that the road from the Swan Inn to the Station Road should retain the name of Swan Road — this being the name by which it has been known for many years past — and to point out to them that the road leading from "The Copse" to the Mill is the only roadway known as Mill Road."

The question of amalgamation with Yiewsley had been discussed many times. In 1924 there was strong opposition to a proposal that both West Drayton and Yiewsley should form part of an enlarged Uxbridge Urban District. Further discussions then took place on uniting West Drayton and Yiewsley which resulted in the formation of the Urban District of Yiewsley and West Drayton. There was strong opposition from West Drayton at the choice of title for the new authority, for they felt, with some justification, that as West Drayton was by far the older parish the title should have been West Drayton and Yiewsley Urban District.

The new council began operations in 1929 with a staff of five housed in the old Working Men's Club building in Yiewsley High Street. Later it appointed a rating officer at a salary of £360 per annum, rising by annual increments of £10 to £400. A motor driver was engaged at £3. 10s 0d (£3.50) a week.

The council was in urgent need of more suitable offices and obtained the Minister of Health's sanction to borrow £6,000 for sixty years for this purpose. The new Town Hall was erected on the site of the old offices and was opened by Councillor F. E. Dominey, Chairman of the Council, in May, 1930. The council was soon active in providing additional recreational facilities for the whole district. In 1933 it considered plans for the open air swimming pool at an estimated cost of £2,800 and the following year came the provision of tennis courts (derelict in 1982) in The Closes.

When the newly formed council took office in 1929 the rates were 14s 2d (71p) in the pound. Ten years later, just before the outbreak of the Second World War, the rate was 14s 0d (70p), despite the fact that provisions had now to be made for air raid precautions costs.

SOCIAL LIFE

Although many of the old type of local entertainments, such as school or church concerts and pantomimes, resumed after the first World War, the advent of the cinema and broadcasting brought about a considerable change in the way that people spent and enjoyed their spare time.

When the war ended, sporting events continued in much the same way as they had before 1914. There were cricket and football clubs, the most prominent being West Drayton Cricket Club and Yiewsley Football Club. The cricket club went through a very successful era. In 1929 the 1st XI scored 283 runs for three wickets against Upper Tooting before declaring, while on May 7th 1933 R. O. Stone took all ten of India Gymkhana's wickets for only thirty runs.

In 1924 residents of the new Garden City Estate formed their own cricket club. Known originally as Garden City Cricket Club, but in later years as Yiewsley-Drayton, its ground was at Thorney next to the Staines branch of the railway. At the club's annual dinner held in the Regal Restaurant, Uxbridge in 1935, the guest of honour was the England and Middlesex all-rounder, J. W. Hearne, who later lived at 16, Bagley Close, where he died in 1965.

In 1925 a short-lived Constitutional Club was opened in the former Baptist Chapel in Money Lane, which had been renamed Frays Hall. Then in 1928 came the West Drayton Players, formed by the sisters Peggy and Maud Ross of De Burgh Crescent, who had had professional acting experience. The West Drayton Players were still performing for a short period after the Second World War. They gave many excellent performances throughout the district, mostly in aid of charity. The West Drayton & District Canine Society had a short life in the 1930's. In 1935 it held its show in the Railway Arms Hall but the following year chose a more ambitious venue, the Drill Hall in Handel Street, Bloomsbury.

The Marlborough Cinema in Yiewsley High Street was opened by the Chairman of Yiewsley Urban District Council, Councillor F. E. Dominey, in September, 1923 and the first film shown was "Circus Days" in which the boy

An outing from the Brickmakers' Arms in the early 1920's

actor, Jackie Coogan, starred. The Marlborough was an instant success. It had 554 seats, a third of them being in the balcony, and prices ranged from 5d (2p) to 1s 10d (9p). The balcony seats were particularly popular and the cinema's patrons were advised to book their seats in advance at the sweet shop next door. By 1930 plans were announced to enlarge the cinema and this was completed in 1933.

The cinema and other forms of recreation were affected by the Sunday Observance laws. In 1923 Yiewsley Council decided that its allotments should be closed on Good Friday, the traditional day for planting potatoes. In 1933 a poll was taken as to whether films should be shown on Sundays. 39% of the electorate voted, 1690 being in favour of Sunday opening of the cinema and 890 against. The following year the council banned the playing of bowls and tennis in its recreation grounds on a Sunday and opposed the use of swings in The Closes. There was an uproar over this decision which a special council meeting failed to resolve. Finally, in June, 1935 the Council agreed by eleven votes to nine to allow Sunday games, and instructions were given for the recreation grounds and swimming bath to be opened on a Sunday.

At the time that the Marlborough Cinema was opened a new craze had hit the district. This was radio — or "listening-in" as it was then known. These were the early days of broadcasting, and enthusiasts spent much of their time moving a piece of wire known as a cat's whisker over a small crystal. When the

53

wire contacted a live spot on the crystal the enthusiast would hear the broadcast through his headphones plus a good many squeaks and whistles.

In March 1923 West Drayton Women's Institute met in St. Martin's Hall to hear Mr. Stockwell give a lecture on this new form of entertainment. He had a valve set operated by batteries which enabled him to use a loud speaker, and after the lecture he gave a demonstration. The Institute members were then able to hear "a meeting held at Kingsway Hall and later the selection from "Veronique" played by the Wireless Orchestra. At the close of the evening news was broadcasted, almost every word of which was audible all over the room." Later in the year another demonstration was given in St. Martin's Hall when Mr. S. C. Piper brought his four valve wireless set and loud speaker to the church bazaar.

"Listening-in" had certainly become popular in the district, and Mr. J. Sutton of 47, Acacia Avenue suggested that a wireless society should be formed. By the beginning of April 1923 Yiewsley and West Drayton Radio Society had been established and in July it met at Chapel House in Ernest Road, when Mr. Archer demonstrated his three valve set and Mr. Puddephat his "True Music" loudspeaker. The Radio Society had its practical side, too. By the end of July arrangements had been made to install a new aerial and it was discussing the possibility of building a three valve set.

Fifteen years later another phenomenon had arrived — television — but its full impact on the district could not be known until after the Second World War, for all television broadcasting ceased during hostilities.

THE SECOND WORLD WAR

In the late summer of 1938 it seemed that war was imminent. Loud speaker vans toured the district advising people to collect a gas mask from local schools and work started on digging trenches in the parks and open spaces. The signing of the Munich Agreement brought about a temporary respite, but preparations on air raid precautions were intensified. On Sunday, September 3rd 1939 war was declared on Germany, and while many people were attending the morning church services the sirens sounded for the first time in West Drayton; but fortunately it was a false alarm.

The black-out was imposed immediately. Street lighting ceased and windows had to be heavily curtained during hours of darkness. The district had been divided into sections for air raid precaution purposes and A.R.P. Posts were set up throughout West Drayton and Yiewsley. Fire watching parties were formed to cover every street, and later, when invasion seemed probable, West Drayton Local Defence Volunteers (soon to be renamed the Home Guard) was formed with the local schoolmaster, Guy Butler, as its commander.

The Rev. Leslie E. Prout wrote in St. Martin's Parish Magazine "These days of difficulty may produce unusual circumstances in many homes and I would like to offer my services without regard to creed or church membership, whether it be merely guidance in filling up forms or advice, general or spiritual." It was a difficult time for all the churches. Most of them could not be blacked out, so the times of services had to be altered during the winter months. At St. Martin's the early morning service was altered from 8.15 a.m. to 8.45 and evensong had to be brought forward from 6.30 p.m. to 3.30. The ringing of church bells was banned except as a warning in the event of an invasion. This would have proved

Armistice and Second War 1918-1945

useless, however, had there been an invasion, for the bells could not be heard all over the parish.

Most able-bodied men were callled up for military service and others were directed to war work in factories. Women were also conscripted for war service, and in 1943 a day nursery was opened in Station Road where they could leave their children. Although most people were working long hours, many found time to support the "Dig for Victory" campaign by spending their spare time working on their allotments.

In 1943 a British Restaurant seating two hundred opened in Yiewsley High Street, where a dinner costing 1s 2½d (6p) could be obtained between 12 and 2 p.m. on a weekday. The British Restaurant was not a financial success and when it closed in 1945 there was an estimated loss of £718.

The log books of A. R. P. Post H (which covered most of the present West Drayton Green Conservation Area) have survived and tell much of the problems of West Drayton in war time. The wardens' responsibilities included seeing that the blackout restrictions were not infringed, and at 9.25 p.m. on August 3rd, 1940 Warden Kelvie reported "Electric lights full on outside garage in Mill Road. Police notified at once as proprietor was out. Also called at private house. Nobody at home." Later a man climbed up the post at the garage, removed the bulb from the floodlight and tore the wire out of the petrol sign.

On October 17th, 1940 a policeman called at the post and asked

Digging trenches at Yiewsley

"whether we had seen a bomb drop — said an ambulance driver had just rushed by him shouting that a bomb had fallen on Swan Road. During his visit the cheerful sound of drunken singing could be heard proceeding from the direction of Swan Road. This was pointed out to him, and he withdrew, calmed."

Less than a month later, on November 11th, the first bombs did fall in the area covered by Post H, when an incendiary burnt itself out on the island in Money Lane. Other incendiaries fell on West Drayton during the war, causing fires at the Britannia Works, St. Catherine's Rectory and a house and a tobacconist's shop in Swan Road. A more serious incident occurred when a house next door to the Vicarage in Station Road was so badly damaged by a bomb that it had to be demolished. Fortunately nobody was hurt.

By the late summer of 1944 a new form of aerial attack was hitting southern England — the flying bomb or V1 rocket. At 11.30 p.m. on Saturday, August 19th one of them fell on Pett's Nursery in Wise Lane. The blast from it loosened the stained glass east window in St. Martin's Church and also forced open the front door of a bungalow in Bagley Close. The following day a local resident recorded in his diary. "In the afternoon saw the bomb damage in Wise Lane. It is amazing that tomato plants are still standing in the greenhouses although the glass has fallen on them." A few days later the Vicar's wife, Mrs. E. S. Prout, wrote to a friend in Cornwall:

> "We have had some hectic times lately. One night we made sure it was coming directly down here. The engine stopped and the thing came whistling down. It landed on Pett's greenhouses in Wise Lane. All was destroyed, including the greater part of the bungalow. Fortunately there were no casualties except for one man who got cut on the face. But the whole of 20 years' work has gone including 5 tons of tomatoes. Sunday last was a most trying day. Sheets of rain the whole day and the siren going constantly and continual bumps. One went right across just after the 8.15 celebration [of Holy Communion], it landed somewhere near Denham and another in Langley Park. They make a terrific noise when they come so low. A good many windows have been broken about the village. In Drayton Park Avenue both the Mays and the Gittins had windows broken and ceilings down — Miss Mercer, too, had several of hers broken. In the church four of the small diamond panes in the window by the font were broken. It was indeed a wonderful escape for W.D."

The following May came the German surrender and shortly afterwards that of Japan. The black-out was a thing of the past and street lighting returned. Street parties and celebrations were held everywhere. A bonfire was lit on the small green outside the Gate House and fireworks were let off, which was against the law. While the residents of Church Road and Bagley Close were enjoying themselves a policeman appeared, riding a bicycle. He stopped, dismounted, walked slowly across the road, putting his hand into his pocket. There was complete silence. He withdrew his hand from his pocket and it was noticed that he was holding a Roman candle. "Here's another one for you," he said, and then turned back towards his bicycle.

The long war years were at last ended. But during those years one event had occurred which had passed almost unnoticed, yet which was to have a momentous effect on the future history of West Drayton. In June, 1944, a preliminary announcement was made of plans to build an airport at Heathrow.

Chapter Six

From Village to Suburbia 1945 – 1982

THE EFFECT OF HEATHROW AIRPORT

The opening of Heathrow Airport in 1946 changed the history of West Drayton completely. It provided work for many thousands of people but the demand could not be met from the surrounding area. This meant that thousands of its employees came from other districts and there was thus a great demand for houses in West Drayton. The result was that every available piece of land was built on. The demand for accommodation, however, was so great that it caused the price of land and houses to soar. In 1927 the Gate House and the nursery land at its rear (now Beaudesert Mews) had been sold by the De Burgh Trustees to the Middlesex County Council for £900. The Gate House (but not the nursery land) later passed into private ownership. In September, 1978 the Gate House was advertised for sale in the Daily Telegraph for £55,000. A bungalow in the conservation area, which had cost £725 when it was built in 1928, was in the market at over £40,000 in 1982.

The airport, with the consequent local developments, brought about a vast increase in traffic passing through West Drayton, with which the local roads were unable to cope at rush hours. At times the stream of traffic trying to enter Station Road from Harmondsworth Road stretched back as far as West Drayton Cemetery. In 1982 work started on constructing the Yiewsley Bypass in an effort to relieve the congestion. This may ease the situation partially, but it will not solve the problem completely, for the building of two large private estates in West Drayton and the proposed sale of six acres of council-owned land in Harmondsworth Road to a private developer will mean that still more cars will be starting their journeys within the locality.

On the credit side, the airport and its surrounding hotels have provided much work for the people of West Drayton and Yiewsley. In 1949 West Drayton Labour Exchange could claim to have the lowest unemployment figures in the London region — only seventy registered unemployed out of an estimated working population of seven thousand, and by the middle of 1956 the figure had fallen to twenty-three. In 1947 the urban district council had difficulty in filling vacancies for five dustmen and was obliged to increase the wage for a 47 hour week to £5. 5s 3d (£5.26) plus superannuation as an inducement.

The airport was the largest ratepayer in the urban district, which enabled the domestic rate to be kept lower in comparison with most other areas. However, when the urban district was absorbed in the London Borough of Hillingdon in 1965 the domestic rate rose sharply, for the rates from the airport then had to be spread over the whole of the new borough.

The vast influx of new residents, many of whom only stayed for a year

West Drayton & Yiewsley through the centuries

or two, completely altered the character of West Drayton. It has destroyed the village community spirit which still existed to a certain extent up to the outbreak of war in 1939. Until the mid-1930's it was possible to know most people in the village. 50 years later one can sometimes walk the whole length of Station Road without seeing a familiar face.

LOCAL GOVERNMENT

In 1934 Mr. Hanson offered to sell Drayton Hall to the urban district council but no action was taken. The Town Hall at Yiewsley had been open for only four years and it provided adequate accommodation for the council's staff. Drayton Hall was sold and the new owner continued to use it as a private hotel.

After the war Yiewsley Town Hall was becoming too small to meet the needs of the local authority, and in 1948 the Ministry of Health agreed to allow the council to purchase Drayton Hall for £10,000 plus £540 in legal fees. Eventually Middlesex County Council bought Yiewsley Town Hall for £9000 and a small council office at Heathrow was sold to the Air Ministry for £475.

Drayton Hall, however, was in a deplorable state structurally and its grounds were overgrown. The restoration of the building and its conversion into offices did not begin until 1951 and the work was completed early in the following year. The official opening by the Chairman of the Council, Councillor G. W. Varley, took place on April 5th, 1952. In 1955 an extension to the building was completed at a cost of £6,000.

Late in 1961 the proposal to amalgamate the urban district with the Borough of Uxbridge and the Urban Districts of Hayes and Harlington and Ruislip-Northwood was announced and this was strenuously but unsuccessfully opposed by Yiewsley & West Drayton Urban District Council. The amalgamation came in 1965. The urban district council held its last meeting in March, and on April 1st West Drayton and Yiewsley became part of the vast new London Borough of Hillingdon. At the same time Middlesex County Council was abolished and the county came under the auspices of the Greater London Council.

Local government re-organisation has affected West Drayton and Yiewsley considerably. Reference has already been made to the immediate increase in rates that it brought. There was also a feeling of local government by remote control. Previously a ratepayer could call at Drayton Hall and see any of the council's chief officers without making an appointment, but this was no longer possible. Until the new Civic Centre opened in Uxbridge in 1979 the council departments were scattered in buildings throughout the borough — the planning department, for example, being at one time as far away as Northwood.

Some of the problems caused by the local government re-organisation have gradually been overcome but others still remain nearly twenty years afterwards.

OTHER CHANGES

Apart from the airport and local government reorganisation, other events took place which have altered the life of West Drayton since the end of the war. In 1965 the M4 motorway was opened at the southern end of the parish, thus isolating it from the adjoining villages of Harmondsworth and Sipson. The motorway reduced the amount of traffic along the Bath Road but has tended to increase it through West Drayton, for its Junction 4 entry is at the Cherry Lane roundabout.

From Village to Suburbia 1945-1982

In 1960 the railway bridge was reconstructed and the roadway beneath it lowered to enable double-decker buses to pass under it. Previously lorries with very high loads became wedged under the old bridge and traffic would be held up for long periods. The width of the road was increased to 30 feet and a footpath provided each side, instead of the narrow path on one side as previously.

Under the Beeching Plan the two branch railway lines were closed, that to Uxbridge in 1962 and the Staines line three years later. The Uxbridge branch line was removed but the Staines branch is still used occasionally for commercial traffic. Rail travel was still cheap after the war. In 1954 the first class return to Paddington was 3s 7d (c. 18p) but after 5 p.m. on Mondays to Friday this was reduced to 2s 3d (18p) — and there was a fast train at 5.05 p.m! By paying another 3d (c. 1½p) the journey could be continued as far as Piccadilly Circus on the underground.

By 1971 the Air Traffic Control Centre in Porters Way was established to monitor both civilian and military aircraft flights in southern England. During a seven week strike in 1977 by air traffic control workers, the government ordered Royal Air Force tankers to cross the picket line in order to provide facilities essential for the effective defence of the United Kingdom air space.

1963 saw the opening of Europe's largest coal depot, built at a cost of £400,000, in Tavistock Road. The vast heaps of coal in the depot's yard produced problems for those living nearby when coal dust was blown in their direction during high winds. The coal depot made national news in 1972 when striking miners from Coventry picketed its entrance in an attempt to stop supplies being moved.

West Drayton Mill and the narrow mill bridge posed many problems in the 1970's. By the end of the decade Mill House was being restored and converted into offices. Various plans to develop the derelict mill site were considered over many years; the latest still awaited a decision in the autumn of 1982. In 1976 the council announced its intention to widen the mill bridge and this was strongly opposed by local residents and conservationists on the grounds that any widening of the bridge would result in a vast increase in the number of heavy lorries passing through West Drayton. As the result of a public enquiry held in 1977 the Ministry of the Environment upheld the residents' objections. Later this part of West Drayton was improved considerably by the re-alignment of the road beyond the bridge and the rebuilding of the mill wall to provide both a footpath over the bridge and a view of the mill wheel and the river beyond it.

Many old buildings have vanished, notably The Copse in 1966. It stood at the southern end of The Green on the corner of Money Lane and for nearly a century and a half it was the home of the Batt family. A block of flats now stands in its place.

Several old firms have also disappeared. The Rotary Photographic Co. Ltd. which opened in Colham Mill Road in 1900 was sold in 1951 and Hatton Grove now stands on its site. Johnson's Wax Factory was opened at Colham Wharf in 1919 and closed forty years later when it was employing a work force of 350. Colham Wharf, built in 1796, was demolished in 1982 to make way for an office block, Harrier House. Another old firm, Drayton Controls, closed its Horton Road factory in 1980 with the loss of 350 jobs, while one of Yiewsley's most famous shops, Rudlings Stores, ceased trading in 1982 after seventy-five years when the premises were sold for an office development.

West Drayton & Yiewsley through the centuries

HOUSING

In 1944 there were 1,543 occupied houses in West Drayton and 2,182 in Yiewsley. This number was to be greatly increased with the huge local authority and private developments that have taken place since the end of the second world war. Council estates have been built or extended at Bell Farm, Stockley, Wise Lane, The Glebe and Philpott's Farm. All these developments took place in outlying parts of the district and most of them included a small shopping parade. The Wise Lane Estate even had its own public house, The Cat and Fiddle, which opened in 1956.

Immediately after the war, work was started on building 118 houses on the *Bell Farm Estate* at an estimated cost of £99,000, but by the time these houses were completed two years later this sum had been exceeded by £15,000. Development of another part of Bell Farm was halted by the Ministry of Health in 1945, as there was then a possibility that the houses might be in the path of aircraft should the airport be extended north of the Bath Road. It was not until four years later that work could resume, after the airport plans had been modified.

In 1947 came plans for the development of the large *Stockley Estate* on the derelict site of the old brickfields. Rutters Close, in fact, takes its name from Rutter's brickfield. This estate involved the construction of a wide approach road, Porters Way, which opened in 1951. It replaced a narrow footpath lined by tall hedges which had led to the old brick workings. In the early nineteenth century this footpath had been known as Porters Lane or Portway Lane. A little later work started on the *Philpotts Farm Estate* at Yiewsley, and by March, 1953 the first three of its proposed 263 houses were occupied.

550 houses were planned for the *Wise Lane Estate* in 1953 and work then started on building the first 160 of them. Three years later this estate was being extended by the building of 7 shops with flats over at a cost of £37,292 and 49 small flats on the Harmondsworth Road costing £58,523. By 1954 the thousandth post-war council house had been completed.

Foundations for the houses on the *Glebe Estate* were being laid in 1960 and some of the houses were offered for sale at prices ranging from £2200 to £2750. There was a nominal deposit of £1 and legal costs amounted to £39. At the end of 1963 work commenced on building the final 459 houses on this estate, and also three shops and the Drayton Court senior citizens' flats.

The council provided a good deal of *sheltered accommodation* for the elderly. Franklin House had opened in 1963, to be followed by both Drayton Court and Yiewsley Court in the following year. Then came The Burroughs in 1965. Further sheltered accommodation was built next to Franklin House in the late 1970's. A controversial decision was made in 1952 when the council agreed to provide a ten acre site for caravan dwellers next to the cricket ground.

Under the Labour-controlled Hillingdon Borough Council of the 1970's a good many privately-owned properties were acquired by the council either by negotiation or by means of a compulsory purchase order. In November, 1975 the newly built *Shawfield Court* flats in Church Road were being offered for sale at £14750 each but shortly afterwards they came under council ownership as a result of a compulsory purchase order. When control of the council passed to the Conservatives in 1978 there was a change in policy and many council house tenants were able to take the opportunity of buying their homes at a low price.

Private development has been on a much smaller scale. There have been extensions to West Drayton Park Avenue and Fairway Avenue and also

Facing: Map of West Drayton and Yiewsley, 1982

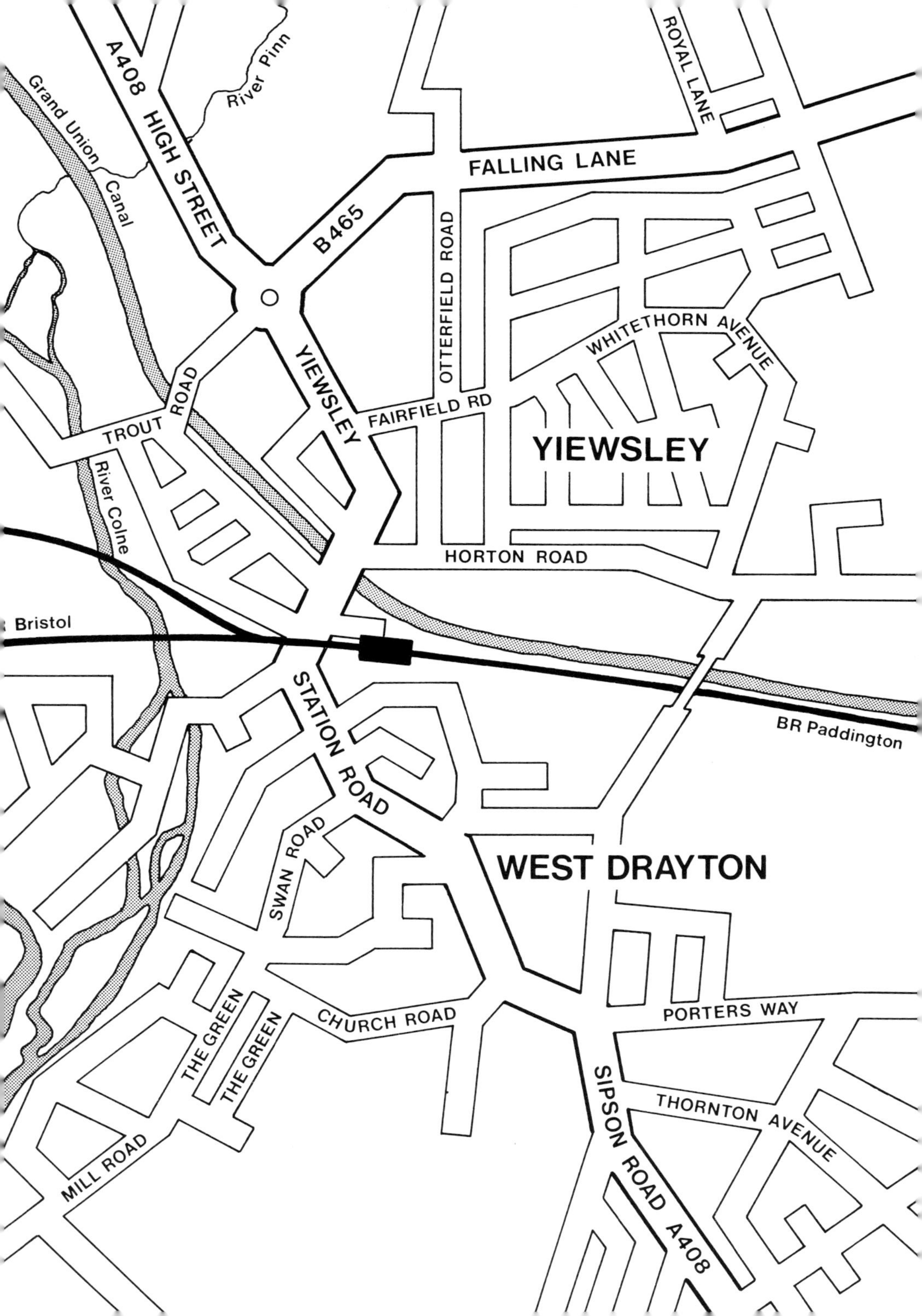
A408 HIGH STREET
River Pinn
Grand Union Canal
ROYAL LANE
FALLING LANE
B465
OTTERFIELD ROAD
WHITETHORN AVENUE
YIEWSLEY
TROUT ROAD
FAIRFIELD RD
YIEWSLEY
River Colne
HORTON ROAD
Bristol
BR Paddington
STATION ROAD
SWAN ROAD
WEST DRAYTON
CHURCH ROAD
PORTERS WAY
THE GREEN
THE GREEN
THORNTON AVENUE
SIPSON ROAD A408
MILL ROAD

some infilling in very large gardens, especially in the Garden City. The post-war years have seen the construction of many small roads such as Caroline Close, Catherine's Close, Frays Close, Copse Close, Mill Close, Roseary Close, Treeside Close, Church Close and Beaudesert Mews. Private developments on a larger scale were taking place late in 1982 on the site of the former primary school in Station Road, in Church Orchard off Church Road and at Philpott's Farm, Yiewsley. Throughout 1982 a proposal by Hillingdon Borough Council to sell six acres of land in the Harmondsworth Road to a private developer met with bitter opposition from local residents, over a thousand of whom signed a petition protesting at the scheme.

AMENITIES

With the rapid growth of the district the need for further amenities became apparent. In some cases this was influenced by national events.

The introduction of the National Health Service in 1948 meant that the local nursing associations were no longer required. They were voluntary organisations and had served West Drayton and Yiewsley well for many years. In 1946 West Drayton Nursing Association had 1,250 members and Nurse Roberts and Nurse Ramsay paid no less than 3,780 visits to 183 patients. The annual membership for a family was only 5s 0d (25p). In 1948 the Health Clinic, which had been located in the Methodist Central Hall, was transferred to the former British Restaurant building. This was replaced in 1971 by the Yiewsley Health Centre which had been built at a cost of £100,000.

The need for a *community centre* was obvious and Oscar Frey, founder of the Anglo-Swiss Screw Company, donated £35,000 towards the cost. When the Padcroft Boys' Home closed in 1949 the building was acquired for use as a community centre by the Middlesex Education Committee for £15,000. By January, 1952 the centre was well established and had a membership of five hundred and sixty. Padcroft, however, was not an ideal building for such a project and in 1965 the new Community Centre in Harmondsworth Road was built at a cost of £90,000. The official opening was performed by Lord Beswick, a former Member of Parliament for Uxbridge, in June, 1967.

In 1964 the Urban District Council had acquired Southlands and agreed to let it to the Yiewsley & West Drayton Arts Council on a seven year lease at a rental of £1 per annum. *Southlands Arts Centre* was opened by Lord Willis, author of the television series "Dixon of Dock Green," on June 3rd, 1967. In addition to providing a meeting place for various local organisations it is frequently the venue for arts and handicraft exhibitions.

For the youth of the district there were the scout and guide troops and also clubs provided by the local churches. The *Yiewsley and West Drayton Boys' Club* was started by Toc H in 1938 and in its early days met in various buildings in West Drayton. During the difficult days of the war it was ably led by Jack Stevenson who resigned as leader in 1948. The club obtained its own premises in 1953 when it was granted a ten year lease on a derelict bungalow in Cherry Lane by the Middlesex County Council at a rental of £1 per annum. The building was renovated and adapted by the club members, and in 1964 a government grant of £13,000 was received towards the cost of erecting a gymnasium in the grounds. In 1969 plans were announced by Hillingdon Borough Council for building a new *youth centre* in Harmondsworth Road costing £57,000. This opened in 1971 and an extension was added in 1982.

From Village to Suburbia 1945-1982

The need for a *police station* in the district had been stressed for many years before the war. West Drayton was served by police from Harlington Police Station but Yiewsley came under Uxbridge. The development of the airport led eventually to the demolition of Harlington Police Station and in 1964 work started on building *West Drayton Police Station* in Harmondsworth Road. Until Heathrow Police Station was built, offences committed at the airport such as drug smuggling were dealt with at West Drayton. When the army was called in during an alert at the airport in 1974 armoured cars were based at West Drayton Police Station's car park.

The old National School in Station Road was demolished in 1961 and *West Drayton Library* was erected on its site. The library cost £17,385 to build and when it opened in 1962 it had a stock of eleven thousand books. It was the last library to be provided by the Middlesex County Council, and it is interesting to recall that the County Council's first full-time library was at Yiewsley in the former Methodist Church building in the High Street. The present purpose-built Yiewsley Library opened in 1973 and the old building was later used for a period as Unit 2 Youth Centre.

Residents on *The Common* had for long had problems over the access to their homes. In 1948 a party of volunteers led by Councillor A. E. Stevenson made up Cricketfield Road, but the real problem was that there was no suitable access for vehicles across the river, which was spanned only by a wooden bridge. The problem became acute when a car breaker's yard opened at the southern end of The Common, and eventually the owner of the business, Mr. A. Odell, erected a bailey bridge over the river beside the footbridge. The bailey bridge was eventually taken over by the council and the wooden footbridge fell into disrepair and no longer exists.

In 1973 *West Drayton Green Conservation Area* was set up, and later an advisory panel consisting of members of various organisations operating within the area was formed. West Drayton Green Conservation Area Advisory Panel is, as its name implies, purely an advisory body and has no power of veto. It meets regularly and comments on such items as planning applications within the conservation area, maintenance of open spaces, traffic problems, landscaping and tree preservation.

Other amenities that came in the years after the war were the extension of the Post Office in 1962, the opening of a car park in Station Road in the late 1960's and the roofing of Yiewsley Open Air Swimming Pool in 1976. This cost £99,000 and took two years to complete.

One other event that can be considered as an amenity to the district was the acquisition of St. George's Meadows in Mill Road by the *National Trust* in 1964. The Tudor cottage and its extensive grounds were bequeathed to the Trust by the late Miss Emily Grigsby. If it were not for her generous act it is more than likely that this pleasant corner of West Drayton would have become an estate developer's paradise.

SCHOOLS

At the end of 1949 Guy Butler retired. He had been a schoolmaster in the district since 1910, spending thirty-eight years at the old West Drayton National School and the remaining two at Evelyns. Yet when he started teaching at West Drayton his intention was to remain for only six months. Two other long-serving and much respected teachers left in 1950. Miss Campbell retired as headmistress of West

Drayton Primary School after twenty four years' service and Mr. S. A. J. McVeigh, headmaster of St. Catherine's School for nearly twenty years, left to take up a similar appointment at Reading.

Work started on building *St. Martin's School* in Kingston Lane, a replacement for the former National School, in April, 1957. The headmaster, Mr. L. Reasey, welcomed his first pupils on September 9th, 1958 and the official opening ceremony of the school was performed by H.R.H. Princess Marina, Duchess of Kent, on December 12th. In 1972 a scheme was announced for the amalgamation of St. Martin's School with the Manor School at Ruislip to form a new Church of England school for the whole borough. This was opposed by parents of pupils at both schools, but without success. At the end of the summer term in 1977 St. Martin's School closed and its pupils were transferred to the new Bishop Ramsey School, Ruislip.

In 1968 *St. Catherine's School* celebrated its centenary. It is one of the smallest schools in the district and perhaps as a result of this its standards of education are good. At one time it took children up to the age of fifteen, but when the Douay Martyrs Roman Catholic School opened at Ickenham it became a primary school.

The third church school, *St. Matthew's*, celebrated its centenary in 1972. It was extended and remodelled in 1968 at a cost of £40,000 and further alterations took place in 1982 when its small assembly hall was doubled in size. In 1979 plans were announced to close the nearby *St. Stephen's Road School* and amalgamate it with St. Matthew's and this was accomplished shortly afterwards.

In 1979 *West Drayton Primary School* moved into part of the former St. Martin's School in Kingston Lane, the remainder of the building being occupied by an adult education centre. The old primary school site in Station Road was later sold for £625,000 and a private housing estate was developed there in 1982.

As well as St. Stephen's Road School another Yiewsley school, *Providence Road*, has closed. There was much opposition to this from the parents, for the pupils were transferred to St. Matthew's and Rabbs Farm Schools and for many of them it meant crossing a busy main road. The school closed on July 24th, 1981 and during its final year it had 38 pupils on its roll.

Four new local authority schools have opened in West Drayton and Yiewsley since the war. The first was *Longmead Primary* in 1955 with Mr. G. Davies as its headmaster. Then came *Townmead Secondary Modern* (headmaster Mr. W. W. J. Etheridge). Although the school opened in 1960, the official opening ceremony did not take place until April 11th, 1962. In 1975 Townmead School became comprehensive. It is interesting to note that both these schools are named after ancient West Drayton fields. Another school which received a local name was *Rabbs Farm*, which opened in 1968 with Mr. R. Chapman as its headmaster. As in the case of Townmead School the official opening was delayed and did not take place until early in 1970. At the same time another Yiewsley school, *Chantry*, was opened.

Two local organisations which are closely connected with education were formed a few years after the end of the war. The Yiewsley and West Drayton branch of the *Workers Educational Association* started in 1952 and holds its classes in West Drayton Library during the winter months. On July 1st, 1949 *West Drayton and District Local History Society* was formed with only six members — H. F. Bateman, A. H. Cox, F. Durrans, H. G. Kerry, S. A. J. McVeigh and M. C.

From Village to Suburbia 1945-1982

Twomey. In 1982 the society's membership was well over a hundred and it was giving active support to schools in the area in the study of local history.

CHURCHES

The churches faced great problems when the war ended. Most of their activities had had to be suspended or curtailed by the wartime difficulties and this often meant starting from scratch again. In addition, the strict building regulations, which continued for some time after the war, caused much-needed repairs to churches and vicarages to be postponed. During 1949 the two Anglican churches were involved in the Mission to London, and it must have been encouraging when there were over two hundred communicants at the Midnight Mass at St. Matthew's that Christmas.

Much has happened at *St Martin's* since 1945. Members of the congregation made a presentation to the Rev. Leslie E. Prout to mark his silver jubilee as vicar in 1953. He died in 1956 and his successor, the Rev. A. H. Woodhouse, arrived at a time when the parish was growing rapidly as the new council estates developed. During his incumbency a new vicarage was built in 1960. In May, 1969 the actor Derek Nimmo opened the new St. Martin's Hall which had been erected on the site of the old Vicarage. In addition, the new church school was erected in the Vicarage paddock.

The Rev. A. H. Woodhouse planned to restore and extend the church and various schemes were discussed for many years. In the end the restoration was carried out during the incumbency of his successor, the Rev. P. D. Goodridge. By that time inflation and the long delays in obtaining planning approval caused all thoughts of enlarging the church to be postponed indefinitely.

The restoration started in September, 1974 and took eight months to complete. During that period Sunday services were held in St. Martin's School hall and weekday services at the Vicarage. The mid-19th century pews in the church were replaced with chairs, and a new floor, heating and lighting systems were installed. The most striking change, however, was to place the altar at the western end of the church instead of its traditional eastern position. This enabled everyone in the church to see the altar but the change did not prove popular with many of the older members of the congregation.

West Drayton Baptist Church celebrated its hundred and fiftieth anniversary in 1977, when many former ministers were present. It is one of the smaller churches in the district but is proud of the part it has played in West Drayton's history since 1827.

St. Catherine's Church had its centenary in 1969 when Cardinal Heenan celebrated mass. Plans were then announced for building a new presbytery and social centre. Cardinal Heenan had spent a day in West Drayton four years earlier, during the course of which he visited St. Martin's Church where he joined the vicar in prayer at the altar.

St. Matthew's Church also had a centenary, in 1959. There were further celebrations in 1978 to mark the eightieth anniversary of the extension of the church in 1898. Another joyful event was in 1963 when Prebendary F. W. Ruffle celebrated his silver jubilee as Vicar of Yiewsley. The church was crowded when he preached his farewell sermon on September 30th, 1973, and some former members of the congregation who had left the parish several years before travelled many miles to be present.

A very special event took place in January, 1947 when some German prisoners of war who were still stationed near West Drayton joined *Yiewsley Baptists* at a communion service. Yiewsley Baptist Church celebrated its jubilee in 1950 and four years later decided to sell its Tabernacle and Manse and to transfer the church to the Sunday School buildings at the other end of Colham Avenue. A new building to house the Sunday School was later erected.

The *Methodists* were faced with financial problems in connection with their Central Hall. Heating and lighting costs were high and the congregation not large enough to fill so large a building. In the late 1960's plans were prepared for the demolition of the Central Hall and its replacement by a smaller church, a supermarket and a church hall above. The new building was opened on February 3rd, 1973 by Miss Chandler, an old member of the church. The preacher on that occasion was the Rev. Dr. Maldwyn Edwards, who had been minister when the Central Hall opened in 1927.

People living on the outlying Bell Farm and Stockley estates were a long way from any of the churches, so a new church, *Bell Farm,* was built to meet their needs. This was a non-denominational church sponsored by the Shaftesbury Society and its first pastor was Mr. Percy Bush. At the time of its official opening in February, 1957 its Sunday School already had 320 pupils enrolled.

Perhaps the most important aspect of church life in West Drayton since 1945 has been the effect of the ecumenical movement. This first became evident at the united Coronation service held in the grounds of Drayton Hall in 1953. Later on the churches were drawn much closer together by the efforts of the Rev. A. H. Woodhouse of St. Martin's and the Rev. Howard Booth and the Rev. Ewart Wilson of Yiewsley Methodist Church.

On Good Friday 1965, members of local churches joined together in a procession of witness through West Drayton and Yiewsley, and later that year the *Yiewsley and West Drayton Local Council of Churches* (which also includes Harmondsworth and Sipson) was formed. Since then it has been possible for churches of all denominations to co-operate in such matters as Christian Aid Week, conducting services in old people's homes and, for a period, providing a Good Neighbours Scheme. In 1981 came the Local Council of Churches Mission 81, when members of various churches went out in pairs visiting houses in West Drayton, Yiewsley, Harmondsworth and Sipson. The visiting lasted six weeks and the mission ended on Whitsunday with a procession from The Green to Yiewsley Recreation Ground where a performance of the Gospel Road Show was watched by a large crowd. As a result of the mission a Christian centre, Koinonia, was opened at the Methodist Church in May, 1982 to provide an advice and information service for the young unemployed and others.

SOCIAL LIFE

With the end of the war came the return of television and the abolition of petrol rationing. There had been six years of restrictions and when they were lifted people were anxious to enjoy the things they had for so long been denied. Television aerials began to appear on West Drayton rooftops and there was a great demand for new or secondhand cars. The result of all this was that the style of leisure activities changed completely. People were less inclined to make the effort to amuse themselves when they could relax in an armchair and watch the "box" or get down to the coast in about a couple of hours. This and the huge influx of new residents caused the demise of the old village community spirit which still existed in a small way in 1939.

West Drayton Cricket Club survived the war years and was able to field a third eleven, thanks to the generosity of Gordon and Stewart Davey who had paid the cost of laying a new pitch. *Yiewsley Football Club* turned professional in 1958 and joined the Southern League. It moved to a new ground and when the local government re-organisation took place in 1965 promptly changed its name to Hillingdon Borough.

West Drayton Women's Institute celebrated its diamond jubilee in 1979. In 1951 the Institute's hall on the The Green was opened, the generous gift of the Davey family who lived at Southlands, to commemorate Miss Hilda Davey's twenty-five years as President. Later, in 1975, premises for the Middlesex Federation of Women's Institutes were erected in the grounds. The Women's Institute Hall provided an excellent venue for such events as horticultural shows, exhibitions and wedding receptions. The cost of maintenance, rates and insurance eventually proved too great for the finances of the Institute and in 1982 plans were being considered for converting the greater part of the hall into a doctor's surgery with the Women's Institute retaining the remainder for its meetings.

The West Drayton branch of the *British Legion* was formed in 1948 and soon had a membership of a hundred. In July 1949 the Rev. Leslie E. Prout dedicated the Legion's standard at a service held on The Green. In its early days the Legion met in the Railway Arms Hall but in 1965 it announced its plans to build its own headquarters in front of the council depot in Station Road. A women's section was formed in 1968. After new standards had been dedicated the old standards were placed in St. Martin's Church.

The film "Genevieve" was shown at the *Marlborough Cinema* in 1953 and returned two years later. It was of particular interest to West Drayton people, for part of it had been filmed locally and there were shots of the old railway bridge, the De Burgh Hotel and the entrance to Tavistock Road. The Marlborough changed ownership and was renamed The Ritz in August, 1956, but by December, 1957 it was stated to be losing £2,000 a year and faced possible closure. The Urban District Council refused to lend the cinema £1,000 for a period of three years and an appeal was then made to local industrialists. This appeal was strongly supported by the local clergy, and the Vicar of West Drayton, the Rev. A. H. Woodhouse, expressed his concern at the possible closure of the cinema in a television interview.

The Ritz was closed in July, 1958 as a temporary measure. By then the council was willing to make a grant of £200 provided that a similar amount was promised by local firms The cinema re-opened under new ownership on August 4th. There was then a change of policy and continental sex films were screened. This was strongly condemned by the local clergy and in May, 1959 the renewal of the cinema's licence was refused. The Ritz closed in 1960 and was converted into a supermarket.

The *West Drayton Players* resumed their activities after the war with a production of "Quiet Weekend" and two years later celebrated their twenty-first anniversary, but have since disbanded. A local group of *Unity Theatre* was formed in 1945 and continued for four or five years, giving its performances in St. Martin's Hall. The *XXV Club* (whose members came from twenty-five families living near West Drayton Green) gave open air performances of Shakespeare's comedies in the gardens of The Old House and Southlands for

West Drayton & Yiewsley through the centuries

some years. The club still meets informally in its members' homes but no longer lists amateur theatricals among its activities.

A wartime organisation formed in 1943, the Yiewsley, West Drayton and District Choral Society, eventually developed into the *Fairfield Singers,* so named because it held its rehearsals in the Methodist Church in Fairfield Road. The Fairfield Singers gave much pleasure to West Drayton and the surrounding district for many years with concert performances of Gilbert and Sullivan and other light choral music. In recent years there has been a change of policy and choral works of a more serious nature are performed. There has also been a change of name to the Fairfield Choral Society, and rehearsals are no longer held in West Drayton or Yiewsley.

Members of local organisations took part in a nativity play, "Ding Dong Merrily on High" which was performed in St. Martin's Church at Christmas 1968 and 1969. Other performances were given in Christ Church, St. Marylebone and St. Alban's Church, Holborn. The play was produced by Andrew Low of Mill Road. On a much larger scale was his production of the pageant "Gloriana" in the grounds of Drayton Hall as part of the Festival of London in 1972.

West Drayton celebrated Queen Elizabeth II's coronation in 1953 and her Silver Jubilee in 1977. For many years children's sports and town fetes were held in Drayton Hall grounds and carnival processions passed through the streets. These were particularly happy occasions and attracted large crowds, but partly owing to lack of funds they are no longer held.

In 1948 the Olympic Games were held at Wembley and many West Drayton people attended them. Athletes from all over the world were housed in Middlesex and Hertfordshire, those from Brazil and Austria being billeted at West Drayton Royal Air Force Station. The district still looked very shabby after the long years of wartime neglect, and in an effort to brighten it up for the visitors it was decided to repaint the walls of the railway station. The decision was made only a day or two before the teams arrived, so there was not time to clean the walls beforehand and the paint was applied on top of the grime. Fortunately, however, this did not become obvious until after the visitors had left for home.

EPILOGUE

In the summer of 1981 it was feared that the rioting at Brixton would extend throughout the Greater London area and precautions were taken in West Drayton when the danger seemed imminent. A fun fair which had been assembled next to Philpotts Farm, Yiewsley was hastily dismantled and moved away before it had opened and on police advice shopkeepers in Station Road and High Street, Yiewsley barricaded their shopfronts with wooden screens. Fortunately the anticipated outbreak did not occur and the barricades gradually disappeared. One shop in Station Road, however, still protects its entrance with a wooden screen each night.

The two world wars had a big effect on the lives of many West Drayton people, but the Falklands Campaign of 1982 made very little impact locally for it was fought by men already serving in the armed forces and there was no conscription. One young West Drayton man who did serve with the Task Force was Private Jeffrey Moorcroft of the 2nd Paratroop Regiment. He returned safely to see for the first time his baby daughter, Cassandra, who was born on the day he was on active service at Goose Green.

This brief account of West Drayton's history was written in 1982, and little more remains to be told by the present historian, for the effects on the district of the Yiewsley By-Pass and the housing developments, either in progress or proposed, have yet to be assessed. In the course of fifty years West Drayton has changed from a pleasant village into a crowded outer London suburb. Yet despite all the modern developments many fine old buildings still remain to remind us of the history of West Drayton through the centuries.

Sources

Printed works

BAGLEY GARDENS ESTATE	Brochure, c. 1930
CAMDEN MISCELLANY	Vol. XXV
COTTON, Jonathan	Excavations in Church Road, West Drayton, 1979–80: in *London Archaeologist*, vol. 4, no. 5, winter 1981, pp. 121–129
DAILY TELEGRAPH	18.1.1972
DRAYTON HOUSE ESTATE	Brochure, c. 1925
EVENING NEWS	May 1929, advertisement
GARDEN CITY ESTATE	Brochure, c. 1920
JOHNS, A. F.	Music lessons prospectus, c. 1930
LYSONS, Daniel	Historical account of those parishes in Middlesex which are not described in the environs of London. 1800
MacVEIGH, S. A. J.	Drayton of the Pagets. 1970
MacVEIGH, S. A. J.	West Drayton past and present. 1950
MIDDLESEX AND BUCKINGHAMSHIRE ADVERTISER AND GAZETTE	1854–1982
MIDDLESEX SCHOOLS GAZETTE	May 1936
MIRROR OF LITERATURE, AMUSEMENT AND INSTRUCTION	no. 914, 29 September 1838
PIGOT	Commercial directory, 1826
ROYAL COMMISSION ON HISTORICAL MONUMENTS	Middlesex. 1937
SAINT MARTIN'S CHURCH	Magazine 1890–1916
SPERLING, J. H.	Church walks in Middlesex. 1849
SUNDAY TELEGRAPH	6.1.1974
THE TIMES	11.11.1963
VICTORIA HISTORY OF THE COUNTIES OF ENGLAND	Middlesex, vol. 3, 1962
WEST DRAYTON AND DISTRICT LOCAL HISTORY SOCIETY	West Drayton and District Historian, 1958–1982

Manuscripts

ANGLESEY COLLECTION	(Greater London Record Office, acc. 446.)
A.R.P. Post H	Log book, 1939–1944
COX, A. H.	Diary, 1939–1945
CENSUS RETURNS	1861
DE BURGH COLLECTION	(Greater London Record Office, acc. 742.)
HILLINGDON & WEST DRAYTON BRITISH SCHOOL	Annual reports, 1829–1833
PARKER, John A.	Interview (tape recorded)
PROGRAMMES	"Ding dong merrily on high"
	Fairfield Singers
	"Gloriana"
	XXV Club
PROUT, Mrs.	Letter to Miss Ratcliff, August 1944
RATCLIFF, Miss M. F.	Interview (tape recorded)
RATCLIFF, W. J. R.	Diary
SAINT MATTHEW'S SCHOOL	Log book, 1872–1902
VICTORIA AND ALBERT MUSEUM PRINT ROOM	
WEST DRAYTON BAPTIST CHURCH	Records
WEST DRAYTON CHURCHWARDENS' ACCOUNTS	
WEST DRAYTON ENCLOSURE AWARD	1824
WEST DRAYTON GREEN CONSERVATION AREA ADVISORY PANEL	Minutes
WEST DRAYTON NATIONAL SCHOOL	Minute book, 1860
WEST DRAYTON PARISH COUNCIL	Minutes, 1927
WEST DRAYTON VESTRY	Minute book, 1838–1894
YIEWSLEY PARISH COUNCIL	Minutes, 1896–1910

INDEX

agriculture	20
Air Traffic Control	59
allotments	50
Anchor Inn	<u>51</u>
Anglesey, Marquis of	15
Anglo-Swiss Screw Co.	44
archaeology	9, 12
arts centre see Southlands	
Avenue Cottage	14
Avenue House	14,17
Bagley Close	43
Baptists	28, 48, 65-66
Batt, William	20
Beaudesert Mews	12
Bell Farm Church	66
Bell Farm Estate	42, 60
Biscoe, John	15
blacksmiths	<u>40</u>
Bolo, Count see French, George	
brickfields	20-21, 60
Britannia Brewery	17, 20
British Legion	67
British School	24
Burial ground	13, 27
Burnell, family	12, 14
Burroughs, The	10, 12, 14, 15, 60
buses	45
canal	19, 59
Carey, George, Lord Hunsdon	15
Castle Avenue	42
Chantry School	64
charities	15
Cherry Lane	14
Cherry Lane School	46
Cherry Orchard	44
Church road	12
churches	26-30, 48-50, 65-66
see also Baptists, Bell Farm,	
Congregational, Elim Hall, Emmanuel,	
Methodists, Roman Catholics, St.	
Catherine's, St. Martin's, St. Matthew's,	
Salvation Army, Yiewsley and West	
Drayton Brotherhood	
churchwardens	31
cinemas; People's Electric	35
Marlborough	52, 67
Ritz	67
Civil War	15
clothing club	22
coal club	22
Colham, manor of	18
Colham Avenue	34
Colham Wharf	59
community centre	62
concerts	35, 67-68
Congregational Church	50

conservation area	63
Coppinger, Fysh see de Burgh, Fysh	
Coney Piece	14
Copts Corner	14
Cowdrey, George	17
cricket	36, 52, 67
de Burgh, family	18
de Burgh, Fysh	17, 18
de Burgh, Robert	27
Denton, Thomas	19
district nurse	22, 62
Dixon-Hartland, Sir Francis, M.P.	20
Domesday survey	10
drainage	31
Drayton Controls	59
Drayton Court	60
Drayton Field	14
Drayton Gardens	43-44
Drayton Hall	13, 17, 58
Drayton House	43
Eastwood's brickfield	20
Eckersall, James	12
education see schools	
Elim Hall	30
Elizabeth I	14-15
Elkins, Rev. Peter	30
Emmanuel Church	30
Empire Day	35, <u>36</u>
employment	20-21, 44
enclosure	13, 14, 19
Engine, The, beerhouse	19
Evelyns School	46, 63
fair	35, 69
Fairfield Singers	68
Fairway Avenue	42, 60
Falling Lane	42
Ferrers Avenue	43
fete	38
fishing	14
floating school	47, <u>47</u>
football	36-37, 67
Fountain, Edward	20
Franklin House	60
Frays, river	14
Frays Close	14
French, George	37
Garden City	37, 42, 62
Gatehouse	12
General Strike	44
Glebe Estate	60
golf	38
golf course	42
Grand Junction Canal see canal	
Great Western Railway see railway	

72

Green, The	**14, 15, 63**
Hatton, Sir Christopher	15
Hawthorne Moor	14
Haynes, John	17
health clinic	62
Heathlands School	46
Heathrow Airport	**9, 57-58**
Hillingdon, London Borough of	58
Hope Cottage	17
horse racing	37
housing	**41-44, 60**
Hunsdon, Lord *see* Carey, George	
Hyll, Robert	11
Hyll, William	11
industry	**21-22, 44, 59**
inns *see* Anchor _, Engine_, Kings' Head _, Swan _	
Johnson's Wax	59
Justices of the peace	31
King's Head Inn	17
library	63
local government	**31-34, 50-52, 58**
Longmead School	64
manor	10
Manor House	12
; demolished	15
Marshall, Timothy	15
Methodists	**49, <u>49</u>, 66**
mills	**14, 20, <u>37</u>, 59**
Money Lane	14
Mooney, Rev. Andrew	29
motorway; M4	58
Myll Lane	14
Napoleon III, Emperor of France	18
National Trust	**14, 63**
oil cake works	20
Old Cottage	14
Otter Dock	34
Overseers of the Poor	31
Oxeney Moor	14
Padcroft Boy's Home	62
Padcroft College	**23, <u>23</u>**
Paget, Lady Anne	14
Paget, Charles	14
Paget, Sir Henry	14
Paget, Thomas	14
Paget, William	**11, 12, 15**
palaeolithic site, Yiewsley	9
Palmers	14
parish council	**34, 50-51**
parish registers	15
Parratt, James	15
paupers	**21-22**
Philpott's Farm	**10, 60, 69**
police station	63
poor relief	**21-22**
population	18
Porters Way	**14, 60**
post office	**15, <u>16</u>, 17, 43, 63**
Power Plant Co.	21
private schools	**22-23**
Providence Road School	**26, 46, 64**
rabbit warren	14
Rabbs Farm	20
Rabbs Farm School	64
race course	37
railway	**19, 44, 59**
Rickmansworth and Uxbridge Valley Water Co.	31
Roadnight, William	20
roads	**34, 45, 51, 62**
Roman Catholics	**29, 30**
Romans	9
Rotary Photographic Co.	**21, 59**
Row, Rev. A. S.	**27, 48**
Rowtheys	14
Royal Air Force	**41, 59**
Royal Naval Air Service	41
Rutter's brickfield	**20-21, 60**
St. Catherine's Church	**30, 65**
St. Catherine's School	**46, 63**
St. George's Meadows	**14, 63**
St. Martin's Church	**10, 11, <u>11</u>, 12, 14, 26-28, 48, 65**
; memorials	**11, 12, 14, 15**
; vicarage	27
St. Martin's Road Council Estate	42
St. Martin's School	**46, 64**
St. Matthew's Church	**28-29, <u>29</u>, 49, 65**
St. Matthew's School	**24-25, 46, 64**
St. Paul's, Dean and Chapter of	**10-11**
St. Stephen's School	**26, 46, 64**
Salvation Army	**28, 30**
schools	**22-26, 45-48, 63-65**
see also British _, Chantry _, Cherry lane _, Evelyns_, floating _, Heathlands _, Longmead _, Padcroft College, private _, Providence Road _, Rabbs Farm _, St. Catherine's _, St. Martin's _, St. Matthew's _, St. Stephen's _, Sunday _, Townmead _, West Drayton Infant _, West Drayton National _, West Drayton Primary _	
sewage	**31, 42**
Shawfield Court	60
Smith, C. Aubrey	36
social life	**35-38, 52-54, 66-68**

73

Southlands	**14, 17, 62**	West Drayton Mummers	**35**
sports	**36-38**	West Drayton Musical Society	**35**
see also cricket, football, horse racing, golf		West Drayton National School	**24-25, 45, 63**
Starveall *see* Stockley		West Drayton Nursing Association	**62**
Station Road	**45**	West Drayton Parish Council	**50-51**
Stockley	**20, 29**	West Drayton Park Avenue	**44, 60**
Stockley Estate	**60**	West Drayton Primary School	**46, 64**
street lighting	**34, 50**	West Drayton String Band	**35**
strikes	**20-21, 44**	Whitethorn Avenue Estate	**42**
Studds, William	**20**	Wilkins Campbell Ltd.	**21**
Sunday Schools	**28, 29**	Wise Lane Estate	**60**
Swan Inn	**19, 40, 51**	women's institute	**67**
Swan Road	**51**	workhouse	**22**
		Worker's Educational Association	**64**
Thatcher, family	**17**	working men's clubs	**22**
Thorney	**9**	World War I	**38-39, 41**
Thornton Avenue	**44**	World War II	**54-56**
Towney Mead	**14**	Worcester, Roger of	**10**
Townmead School	**64**	Wren, Rev. Michael	**30**
transport	**19, 44-45, 58-59**		
		Yiewsley; origin of name	**9**
Uxbridge, Earl of	**15, 17**	Yiewsley and West Drayton Brotherhood	**30**
Uxbridge Rural District Council	**31, 34**	Yiewsley and West Drayton	
Uxbridge Yeomanry	**18**	Drum and Fife Band	**30**
		Yiewsley and West Drayton	
varnish works	**20**	Silver Band	**35, 50**
vestry	**31**	Yiewsley and West Drayton	
		Urban District Council	**52**
water supply	**31**	Yiewsley Choral Society	**35**
West Drayton; origin of name	**9**	Yiewsley Court	**60**
West Drayton and District		Yiewsley Football Club	**36-37, 67**
Local History Society	**64**	Yiewsley Minstrel Troupe	**35**
West Drayton Cricket Club	**36, 67**	Yiewsley Rovers Football Club	**36**
West Drayton Dramatic Society	**35**	Yiewsley Urban District Council	**34, 51**
West Drayton Infant School	**26**	youth centre	**62**

74

Further Reading

ANGLO-SAXON
 CHRONICLE 894 AD
CHRONICLE OF
 AETHELWEARD 893 AD
COLLINS, Desmond — Early man in West Middlesex, H.M.S.O., 1978
COX, A. H. — A Yiewsley benefactor. West Drayton and District Local History Society, 1970

HAYES AND
 HARLINGTON LOCAL
 HISTORY SOCIETY AND
 WEST DRAYTON AND
 DISTRICT LOCAL
 HISTORY SOCIETY — Heathrow and district in times past. Countryside Publications Ltd., 1979

PACKWOOD, G. F. L. and
 COX, A. H. — West Drayton and district during the nineteenth century. West Drayton and District Local History Society, 1967

PEVSNER, Nikolaus — The buildings of England; Middlesex. Penguin, 1951

WALFORD, Edward — Greater London. Cassell, 1894